Praise for

ERA OF IGNITION

"A personal look at big-picture questions, *Era of Ignition* reminds us how powerful, exhausting, and confusing it can be to go through life as a human woman. A mad, frank, tender, and very good read, written with love by a writer who loves you."

—Amy Poehler, *New York Times* bestselling
author of *Yes Please*

"A raw, gutsy, and exposing memoir unafraid to confront difficult questions in this turbulent time."

—America Ferrera, *New York Times* bestselling
author of *American Like Me*

"A personal call to action that reminds us revolution starts by holding up the mirror. A must-read, candid, coming-of-age story."

—Ayanna Pressley, congresswoman
from Massachusetts

"*Era of Ignition* offers illuminating insights into the changing face of feminism and the continued struggle to overcome the hardening lines of gender injustice. A personal and passionate story about making a world 'that is nourished, healed, and flourishing.'"

—*Kirkus Reviews*

ERA OF
IGNITION

Coming of Age in a Time
of Rage and Revolution

AMBER TAMBLYN

B \ D \ W \ Y
Broadway Books
New York

Library of Congress Cataloging-in-Publication Data
Names: Tamblyn, Amber, author.
Title: Era of ignition / Amber Tamblyn.
Description: First edition. | New York : Crown Archetype, [2019]
Identifiers: LCCN 2018047443| ISBN 9781984822994
(paperback) | ISBN 9781984823007 (ebook)
Subjects: LCSH: Tamblyn, Amber. | Actors—United States—
Biography. | Women—United States—Social conditions—
21st century.
Classification: LCC PN2287.T154 A3 2019 |
DDC 791.4302/8092 [B] —dc23
LC record available at https://lccn.loc.gov/2018047443

ISBN 978-1-9848-2299-4
Ebook ISBN 978-1-9848-2300-7

Printed in the United States of America

9 8 7 6 5 4 3 2 1

First Paperback Edition

For Marlow Alice Cross.

And my mother, Bonnie,
and my sister, China.

1

On the bar in front of me, a tea candle meekly flickered at the end of its wick as I sat next to my husband and wondered how I was going to tell him what I had to tell him. We had just gotten married two months before; it was 2012 and we were enjoying the world of newlyweds, our life together on its new trajectory. But my life alone was flatlining. A tire spinning in the mud. A roller-coaster car stuck upside down in midair. I swiveled the ice cubes in my glass full of bourbon and stared down the candle's croaking ember. *That's me,* I thought. *That's me right there in the form of fading fire.*

The flame dwindled as I gulped down my bourbon and proceeded to tell my husband that I was pregnant but was planning to terminate the pregnancy.

I'll never forget the look on his face, a shattering I had instantly caused; a spark of joy pummeled into anguish. He was devastated in that moment, destroyed and blindsided. I cannot remember any other time in my life when I had inflicted this type of pain on another person, especially a person who I loved so much and who was—is—my entire world. I didn't want to hurt him. But I made the choice because I didn't want to hurt anymore either. I had been experiencing a long-term devastation that was omnipresent; an all-consuming, all-encompassing kind of grief. I had come to the end of one very long chapter of my life as a child actress, and now as an adult I was fully out of inspiration and devoid of direction. I was twenty-nine years old and completely lost, lost in a way that I couldn't see a future for myself, lost in a way that isolated me from others. Lost in a way that felt permanently perilous.

I had spent so much of my young life in the entertainment business performing the moments of other people's lives as an actress. The only thing I had ever known how to do was channel someone else's art, be someone else's muse, live someone else's life, speak someone else's words. I began my career when I was just nine years old, acting in a few low-budget films, and by the time I turned eleven, I landed a major role on the soap opera *General Hospital,* a job that would last seven years. While other teenagers were going to school to get an education, I was going to a film studio to play a heroin-addicted former model whose mother had died of cancer. After I left that show at the age of seventeen, I guest-starred in a few TV shows like *Buffy the Vampire Slayer,* then I landed a starring role in the cult TV show *Joan of Arcadia* and didn't stop working, or stop to think about stopping working, for the next ten years.

This is not to say I had a bad childhood; I just had a confusing one. When you've spent your whole life pretending to be other people for a living, it is sometimes hard to know what you are capable of becoming or what you will want once you've stopped. So here I was sitting in a bar, a grown woman who owned a house and a car and had a damn good man in my life, and yet I had absolutely no motivation for living anymore. I was in a deep psychic holding pattern with no sense of what was coming next or who I was. I didn't want to literally die, but I was craving some kind of existential ceasing. I desperately needed to find a way to stop and then to start over again. And I knew that life couldn't stay the way it had been for me, that I had so much more to offer besides auditioning for acting roles. But what I had been experiencing was a sort of invisible alphabet: I saw my life at *A* and could see the bright, glowing *Z* of my potential in the distance but couldn't manifest the letters in between to get there.

In my early twenties, years before I got married, I could feel the dawning of my own personal doom.

I could feel myself starting to come undone. The identity cast I had spent years plastering for myself was beginning to crack, and suddenly the things that defined me were no longer feeding me. I would go into auditions half-assed, half-caring, half-prepared. When I was twenty-eight, I went in to read for the director of a film starring Meryl Streep and couldn't seem to retain a single line of the short monologue I had prepared from the script. Normally I would've excelled in a situation like this. But this time, my body and my mouth wouldn't let me tell this story that was not my own. I began to sweat and could only tell the director I was sorry. "Don't worry," he said to me kindly, "take your time."

Taking my time wasn't the problem, though. My relationship to myself and the world was the problem. Being a lifelong object for a living was the problem. Creative stasis was the problem. I left the audition and broke down in tears in the elevator, shaking and confused. When the doors opened onto the lobby, an actress who looked just like me stepped in as I stepped out, neither of us saying a word to each other, like two mirrors reflecting a single, hollowed-out body.

Things were bad and seemed to only be getting worse. A few weeks after the audition experience, on the eve of my wedding, my agency of fifteen years dropped me as a client. My agent was extremely apologetic, saying she didn't even realize it was the weekend of my wedding. Let this tell you everything you need to know about how invested she was in me. Moments later, my fiancé, David, came into my office, and I couldn't bring myself to look him in the eye. "You shouldn't be with me," I told him with tears dribbling down my chin. "You should be with someone who has their shit together." He held me tight and said, "Honey, Salma Hayek is already married, you know that."

Being dropped by that agency was just one bulb on the string of burned-out lights that felt like it was becoming my life. That night, dejected, humiliated, and drunk, I went through my closet and grabbed a pair of the most expensive high heels I owned and carried them out to the East River near where I lived in Brooklyn. I stared at the long sharp stilettos in shiny patent leather. I had spent so much money on these stupid heels because I was told by a stylist that I should. I didn't even know if I liked high heels. Was this how I liked to dress, or was this just how other people had always liked to see me dress? Everything I thought I knew about myself felt like it was crumbling, breaking apart into tiny question marks. Ceremoniously and rather dramatically, I took these meaningless shoes, artifacts of my artifice, and threw them into the water, one by one, each an unsure wish for a nameless future.

"Dear Shoe: Grant me the strength and wisdom to get through this bewilderment. Dear Other Shoe: I don't want to be just an actress anymore. I want to direct movies and write novels and polish Beyoncé's belt buckles. Please, Other Shoe. Help me help myself."

I staggered toward a nearby monument in the park and pulled my pants down to pee on a statue celebrating some famous man's war. A woman jogged by and pretended not to notice me and my face, a Rorschach test of mascara, crouching and pissing on a giant bronzed replica of a cannon. "Sorry," I muttered while peeing as the woman passed me, "I couldn't hold it in anymore."

Sitting with David at the bar that night a few months after our wedding, I explained with aching clarity what else I couldn't hold in anymore. How unprepared I was, on any level, to bring a child into the world and be responsible for that child. I explained that I was afraid of what kind of parent I would be, or, worse, couldn't be. I was scared that I would subconsciously place blame on the baby for taking me away from my career or that I would harbor some strange jealously for my child, who would have the normal childhood I never got to have. That I would take out all my bullshit on that kid, that I would hate myself for it and, in turn, hate the child, too. I had work to do—a lot of it—before I could be the mother I was capable of becoming. Before I could be the woman I was destined to become. David was supportive and understanding but still heart-shattered.

After I terminated the pregnancy, David and I

did not speak for weeks. I didn't blame him for that; I didn't want to speak to me either. If I could've temporarily exited my own body, I would've. I would've abandoned myself right then and there. But I took morbid comfort in knowing I was going to be the best at my own self-hatred, that there was no one in the world who could hate me more than I could at that moment. At least I was successful in that. At least I was succeeding at hate.

I spent the next month grieving heavily for the loss of many things, both tangible and ungrasp-able, a culmination of my identity, my career, my happiness, and my failed motherhood. I lopped off six inches of my hair with a pair of kitchen scissors as David tried to disappear into our couch, avoiding me. I bought myself some balloons and tied a lock of the hair to one of them with a note that said, "May a witch find this and cast the kindest of spells." I spent evenings combing over the comments section of my IMDb page, seeking the worst possible things people had written about me and telling myself they were all correct: I *am* fat. I *am* a has-been. I *am* the best char-acter in *The Sisterhood of the Traveling Pants*.

MY TURBULENT TWENTIES were not particularly unique. Most people go through personal upheaval when entering the boxing ring of their early thirties. It is a period often described as a Saturn Return, which in astrological terms means the time at which Saturn completes its lengthy trip around the sun, returning to the exact position in its orbit at the point of one's birth, approximately twenty-nine-and-a-half years later. When Saturn returns to these same coordinates, it is believed that those born at this time experience a sort of secondary birth—an existential awakening—that resurfaces the volatility and turbulence of entering into the world in the first place as a newborn.

Why Saturn and not, say, Uranus, where better jokes about the universe being an asshole can be inserted into our daily mythology? The answer lies in the fact that Saturn is more than nine times the size of planet Earth and is encircled by seven astonishing rings that contain more than 150 moons and moonlets (mini-moons!) along with trillions of pieces of ice and dust. Think about how much swagger our own moon has—dictating tides, love songs, and our periods—so imagine a planet with more than 150 of them at its beck and call. Saturn is considered to be the planet most entrenched in wisdom because its long, slow orbit means more quality time spent in each house of the zodiac, richly absorbing its surroundings. Specific energy is created at exact moments when planets align at any given degree—and the energy that is created is you.

So what does it mean to be going through a Saturn Return? One of my best friends, poet and psychologist Mindy Nettifee, says: "It means going through an extraordinary upheaval, initiating a person into finally becoming their adult self." My mother would describe it as "When things start to get real, real fast." And my Jungian therapist, Evan, told me, "Most people in our culture would say one must apply discipline to pulling oneself out of the muck. I would say the muck is where the magic is. One must apply discipline and self-control in staying put and tolerating the difficulties that come with the dark stuff, so that one can be changed and improved by it. Saturn Return is full of opportunity, psychologically."

Psychological opportunity is such a perfect term to describe this time in one's life. To me, Saturn Return is a quarter-life can of whoop-ass. It's when the physical, emotional, psychological, and spiritual dimensions of a person's life all get together in a room and realize they've been cheated on, for years, by reality. It is a metamorphosis of identity, an implosion of self-examination, a coming to terms with a *come to Jesus,* a reckoning with what is simply no longer working anymore. It's a person's candle burning at its lowest, about to go out, unless some new form of flame is found to ignite.

While I have a lot of experience with my own personal Saturn Return over the years, it has become clear to me that our country has been going through one of its own, too. This idea of self-reflection leading to an awakening and rebirth is not unique to the individual's journey, but the journey of a whole consciousness as well.

A crisis of character is nothing new for the United States of America and its long history of abuses of power. When I look at our country today, I see a nation deep in the terror of its own retooling, stuck between a past it can't outrun and the trajectory of a future it must outgrow. We are a nation that still cannot wrap its head around the overwhelming inequality among genders and races in our society and institutional systems. We are a nation that cannot agree on the definition of misogyny, let alone put a finger on its pervasiveness or manifestation. But there seem to be benchmark eras in our history that have brought great and radical change to fruition—times when we weren't just living through difficulties, but actively confronting our values and agitating for revolutionary change. I believe we are in one of those eras right now.

Feminism, for instance, entered its third wave in the early nineties with the emergence of riot grrrl groups led by the likes of Kathleen Hanna touting their punk-rock freedom of expression and creativity. And while some say the fourth wave began a decade ago with the rise of social media, I actually think it's happening right now, in this very moment . . . almost twenty-nine years after that third wave.

What do we call the existential death precipitated

by a Saturn Return and the subsequent rebirth? I call it an Era of Ignition, which is a direct result of and response to our personal and national Saturn Returns. It is a thriving time of condensed evolution, where many discourses about who we are and the difficult dialogues about where we are going kick into high gear. It is an age when activism becomes direct action, when disagreement becomes dissension, when dissatisfaction becomes protest, when accusations become accountability, and when revolts become revolutions. If a Saturn Return asks the difficult questions of one another and ourselves, then an Era of Ignition fires up the answers.

I was once that young woman, answerless and adrift; a soul without a mission. Through my own radical evolution and a stoking of my life's flames, I was able to climb out of the dark abyss I had been engulfed in for so long. I emerged forceful and unafraid and ready for whatever the world had in store for me, but also ready for whatever I had in store for the world. And without America's existential crisis and the questioning of its own values and future, there would be no place for women like me to experience such growth. Without this kind of reflection, there can be no remediation. It is this deep questioning and mining of the problems facing our country that has resulted in the important formation of organizations like March for Our Lives and the Women's March, and for the advancement of those who are not

white and cis. Our nation's Era of Ignition is creating space for important conversations about identity,
race, and gender in ways we have not witnessed in a
very long time: from 2017's #MeToo movement and
women getting together to decide their own fates,
to the power of the Black Lives Matter movement,
to the expansion of pronouns and language used to
define the LGBTQIA community. Our national Era of
Ignition has given voice to people like Laverne Cox
and Hannah Gadsby, Tarana Burke and Alexandria
Ocasio-Cortez. And somewhere in there, by growing out of my role as just a girl for hire and becoming
instead a woman who prospered, my own voice has
been awakened anew. A voice sparked by our nation's
existential engulfment. A voice ignited and burning
for transformation.

2

was sitting at my desk in the East Village apartment I shared with then-Boyfriend David in 2008, five years before he would become Husband David. I was twenty-five and the world felt rich with momentum. Spring had just flexed its muscles, and New York City's ripe smells of Gallery pear trees, toasted bagels, and garbage floated through our open window. The joyous screams of children in the elementary school that neighbored our building rang through the walls. To some this sound can be grating, but I've always found it extremely comforting: a pack of wild young mouths so free and loud, wholly unaware of the turbulence of adulthood.

I had just finished reading Janet Fitch's extraordinary novel *Paint It Black* for the third time and was holding it against my chest, staring out at the fly-sized planes whispering across the sky. Something about the book lingered with me in a way that novels hadn't before. It was as if the book hadn't finished and its story was still a page turning inside me. I could feel an unnameable idea forming in the same way that poems often formed for me—as if being sieved from some larger pulp of ideas. *This novel is a film,* I thought to myself. Moments later, a blaring bell rang out, calling all the kids in from the yard, and it struck me: this novel was not just meant to be a film but meant to be a film of my own making.

What came next was a familiar feeling for most women who step outside of their comfort zones—a pang of fear. How would I get the rights to the book? Who would let me write the movie? Who would I get to direct it? What if my agents just shined me on? What if everyone said no to me? I was surrounded by *what ifs,* instantly consumed by the improbabilities instead of the possibilities.

Hillary Clinton wrote in her memoir *What Happened*—and I'm paraphrasing here—that when she was a partner at the Rose Law Firm in Arkansas and would promote men, they would always say, "Thank you so much for the opportunity. I won't let you down." But when she would promote women, they would often say, "Thank you so much for the opportunity. Are you sure?"

Being unsure seems to be the only framework most women have to see their bigger picture. Women are raised to doubt first and decide last. By this I mean that we question our value or qualifications first, and if we feel that we have not just anything but *everything* to offer, only then do we feel safe to act. For most men, often the opposite is true. They learn on the job. Women learn, triple-check to make sure they've learned, get testimonials and recommendations of their learning, prove a second time that they did, in fact, learn—then they're on the job.

The producer Audrey Rosenberg once told me that women are taught to confuse intuition with anxiety, and I believe this is true at any age. We are kept off-balance in so many ways—like being told that rational thought is the only approved way of thinking and that emotional intelligence is a hindrance, a crutch on which women alone exercise their drama. We are asked to ignore our intuition lest we come off as crazy or hysterical. We are made to see ourselves and our lived experiences as almost cartoonish stereotypes of our truths, which is a way of othering us from our own existence. We are told what roles we can play in society, at home, or in any given profession, and if we try to break out of those roles, we must first hunt for some amorphous permission granted predominantly by most men.

I say "most men" because men, by a wide margin,

run the world; they are largely the ones in positions of power. And the men in those positions, the ones who want to keep their power for themselves, are the ones I am referring to throughout this book. Women are passed over for promotions, jobs, scholarships, or public office because of deeply ingrained biases against our voices, bodies, and perspectives. We say we have the right to choose and decide the laws that pertain to our own bodily autonomy but are then told in the same breath "Nah. You don't." When we speak out against these injustices, we are ignored and told our voices irritate the ear. Our memories are gaslighted and our reputations torched. Our art is rejected and our livelihood diminished. More often than not, men are the gatekeepers and women are locked outside, doing everything we can and sometimes things we don't want to do just to unlock the gate, let alone get a set of our own keys.

Based on what I've written and because I call myself a feminist, a person once asked me if I hated men. (A lot of people say this about feminists in general.) I do not hate men at all. I am critical of them, which is something I wish they themselves would be: have some introspective inquisition. I do not take pleasure in having to police the intentions of these men and this culture as a whole, nor does any other woman I know. It is exhausting and frustrating, leaving little room for the work I would much rather be doing. The notion that I or any other woman takes pleasure in having to continuously point out these grievances is ludicrous and feels more like a ploy to point the finger back at us instead of accepting some responsibility. It is within a man's power to help shift the paradigm, not just a woman's duty to point out the problems inherent in that paradigm. The only way for any of us to be not just part of the problem but part of the solution is to first go inward and observe our own patterns. To own them, then take action.

My own husband is not immune to falling into this category, like most of "most men" I know. They don't think about the ramifications of things they've said or done because they've never had to. But one thing I know to be true about David is that he has always been a strong learner from his mistakes; he will always engage in conversation to gain a better understanding in the hopes that proactivity will come from it. He has long been a champion for women in our business, supporting and amplifying the careers and voices of comedians, writers, and even actresses like myself. So when I told him I was ready to adapt and direct my first feature film, he couldn't have been more encouraging and supportive.

AFTER CALLING MY AGENT and manager to tell them my plans for *Paint It Black,* David and I headed out to get a celebratory drink at our local bar, 2A. We mused about our futures, lives that were beginning their merge toward permanence. I was wearing my black skinny jeans, which were almost painted onto me I wore them so much, and David was wearing a faded T-shirt that read SHREVEPORT IS A SHITHOLE. (If you are from Shreveport and reading this, I apologize for the verbal abuse of your city, which I hear has grown tremendously over the last several years. But you cannot deny that at one time, Shreveport was, in fact, a hole of poop.)

A year earlier, David and I had unexpectedly found ourselves spending time together in the Pelican State while filming two separate movies in the same town. I was traveling to Shreveport on a connecting flight from Houston when I sat down, looked across the aisle, and saw David sitting in the same row. A woman in army fatigues sat in the seat between us, and I tried not to disturb her while attempting to get his attention.

"Hey," I whispered. "HEY, YOU."

He wouldn't look up.

"DAVID. COMEDIAN DAVID CROSS."

The soldier hugged her camouflage bag to her chest, making room for my words to reach him. Begrudgingly, he pulled his eyes out of his magazine, likely thinking I was some superfan ready to accost him. (I kind of was.) He didn't recognize me right away, nor should he have. We had met only a handful of times at industry parties and award shows. A few years before this moment, his *Arrested Development* costar Portia de Rossi had tried to set us up on a date, to which David said, "The girl who talks to God on that CBS show? No thanks." (Shout-out to Portia—we eventually won, girl.)

"Oh. Hi. Amber, right?"

"Yeah!"

". . . Why the hell are you going to Shreveport?"

"I'm judging a mayonnaise competition there."

It wasn't that funny a joke, but it did elicit a small chuckle. David has one of the most infectious laughs of anyone I know. I love it so much. Most people who have come to know me over the years have assumed I got funnier because I'm with a comedian. The truth is I've spent so many years seeking a laugh out of David that I've become funnier out of sheer practice. David didn't make me funnier. I just grew more determined to make him laugh.

"Are you here working on this movie I'm doing, too?" he asked.

"*Beyond a Reasonable Doubt* starring the great Michael Douglas?" I said.

"No," he said, "*Year One* starring the great Jack Black."

"Ah. That's the guy from the thing."

"Actually you're thinking of the guy from that other thing. Jack is the guy from the thing starring those other guys from that one thing."

"Oh shit! You mean the thing about the guy that was in stuff."

"Yes! Wait. I'm lost."

The captain came on over the speaker to let us know we'd be departing soon, and the woman in fatigues asked if I'd like to switch seats so I could sit next to him. *Yes* was the only word I had ever known.

3

As months unfolded into years and we left the East Village for Brooklyn, I started to realize that some of those initial *what ifs* were turning out to be *what nows.* The road ahead was paved with blocks, and not just for my potential film adaptation but for my writing career as well. While trying to get the rights to *Paint It Black,* I had also spent almost five years writing *Dark Sparkler,* a book of poetry exploring the lives and deaths of child star actresses. The book featured original artwork by artists such as Marilyn Manson, David Lynch, and my father, actor Russ Tamblyn, to name a few. The artwork served as an interpretation of the male gaze; male artists interpreting a group of female interpreters (actresses) and their stories. The book closed with an epilogue and a series of meta poems and afterthoughts on what it was like as an actress to write about the brutal deaths of other actresses my own age. The book was an examination and a reflection. An existential death and a resurrection.

It was also unsellable. Month after month I would take it to publishers who would turn it down, saying they just didn't know what the book was—was it a poetry book or an art book? One such editor, who is a friend, wrote me to tell me he couldn't get his company to buy it as they had already purchased a famous male actor's poetry book, due out later that fall. I love that editor very much and his email was filled with sincere regret, but I'll never forget that moment, receiving a rejection based on a comparison like that. I was on vacation and instantly broke down in tears right there on the beach. I cried so much and for so long, my thighs burned from the sun and turned a dark red, with little white splotches where the teary sunscreen had dripped off my face and tie-dyed my legs. I spent the next week looking at my polka-dot cellulite, a constant reminder of my failure.

Why are works by women compared to works by men and rejected based on that comparison? I recently pitched a docu-series with a premise that looks at the language used throughout American history to define women. I was told that the premise was too similar to another program they had already bought where a famous male rapper talks to different people about what is or isn't considered "cool."

What?

Even my mother, a singer-songwriter for more than forty years, who plays a twelve-string guitar and can belt out songs with the best of them, is constantly compared to the likes of Neil Young and Willie Nelson rather than to a famous woman singer songwriter. My sister, China, was in a beloved punk band in San Francisco in the '90s called The Kirby Grips, and they were constantly compared to Nirvana, even though they were far more reminiscent of Hole. These comparisons also reveal themselves in less overt yet equally toxic ways, often appearing in the form of coded terminology that is used to describe works by women that would never be used to describe works by men—terminology that sends a subconscious pronouncement to society about how it is to be valued. My friend, playwright Halley Feiffer, once had her brilliant, hilarious play *A Funny Thing Happened* . . . described in a review for the *New York Times* as "catty." A whole play by a female playwright, not just a single scene, written off with a term that reeks of sexism.

Some of my other favorite sexist terms to describe works by women are "sophomoric," "sentimental," or "quirky." When was the last time you saw a half-hour comedy about men, written by men, that was described as "quirky"? It is the cumulative application of language like this that sends the message to consumers that art by women is to be seen as universally juvenile and immature, whereas art by men can have a chosen juvenilia and immaturity, should their work be intentionally doing that. Using criteria that heavily favor the styles of works by men is a way of branding art by women as beneath the art of men, which is reflected financially in the lesser earning potential of women compared to men. A study for the University of Luxembourg found that fine art by women sells for 47 percent less than fine art by men. One of the reasons women artists have a particularly hard time being taken seriously or selling their work is because of the perceived lack of demand for what we create.

It's no wonder that women are expected to write and think and talk like men in order to be accepted or revered. Women from the Brontë sisters to J. K. Rowling have had to write under male pseudonyms in order to be taken seriously in the literary world. I myself was once told by a famous older male poet at a fund-raiser, among a group of our peers, that I should write under a pseudonym if I wanted anyone to take my writing seriously. What is most disturbing about this comment is that he meant it with no malintent, he just thought this was truly good advice to impart. He thought I would be grateful for this perspective, a perspective that is asking me to literally disappear.

Women have been going undercover as men for more than just artistic reasons. They have had to do it to participate in everything from sports to wars, most famously in the fifteenth century, when Joan of Arc heard voices from a saint who told her to disguise herself as a man in order to fight with other men in the Hundred Years' War. Perhaps that saint whispering in her ear was the eighth-century Saint Marina, who disguised herself as a man so that she could enter a monastery and secretly study and practice as a monk under the male alias Marinus.

Even women athletes have had to pretend to be men in order to compete. Kathrine Switzer famously ran in the Boston Marathon in 1967 disguised as a man because women were not allowed to participate. And before her, in 1959, a woman named Rena Kanokogi once pretended to be a man in order to compete in the YMCA judo championship—and she won. She was forced to forfeit once judges found out her gender, but nevertheless, Kanokogi went on to create the first ever Female Judo World Championship and even coached the first US Olympic Women's Judo Team.

Many black and brown women I know have had their voices rejected in favor of the voices of white women as well. This has never been more apparent than in the casting of television and film. A girl-friend of mine who happens to be black recently told me a story about a film with a phenomenal storyline and great cast that she had been working to put together for more than a decade. "It finally occurred to me that this movie was never going to get made without a white girl in the lead. So I pulled out, because I wanted the film to succeed." Sure enough, a few months later it was cast with a lovely young blonde actress in her role.

Until recently, black and brown women were rarely seen in leading roles in television and film, and if they were, they usually appeared as supporting cast. Asian American women have been virtually nonexistent in leading roles, and the same goes for other minority representation in Hollywood. With all the advancement of equal representation in the entertainment business, this still remains overwhelmingly true today, save for a few films and TV shows, such as *To All the Boys I've Loved Before* and *Crazy Rich Asians,* both of which were massive critical and financial successes. Development and distribution companies seem only to just now be grasping that the success of these movies and TV shows is not merely some lucky coincidence—it is the craving of fresh stories by the American consumer. Yet all kinds of different voices and faces are being left out of mainstream leading roles. As my friend said, "They hire us for recurring roles so they can pay us less money, but then they just put us in all the episodes anyway, as if we should be grateful to have work in the first place." Non-white women have also been left out from behind the camera, with positions for female directors going overwhelmingly to white women directors, no matter how few directing opportunities there are for women overall.

Do works by men get compared to those by women, and do they get rejected based on their similarities? This is a question for men to ask themselves. The answer is likely no. Men's work is compared to other works by their male peers. If you are a man reading this book, ask yourself this question no matter what industry you are in: When was the last time something you made, did, or said was compared to the work of a woman? Go on. I'll wait.

MY ATTEMPTS TO ADAPT *Paint It Black* seemed like an uphill battle against people who saw me solely as an actress, as nothing other than what I had done in the past. I certainly was not seen for what I am: an industry professional with two decades of experience who is capable of writing and producing her own project. Janet Fitch's representatives were extremely hesitant to let me option the book. "Has Amber done anything like this before? Does she have any experience?" the agent asked. I wondered if he would've held a man with the entertainment business tenure I had to the same expectations.

My own agency at that time also seemed wholly disinterested in my new creative pursuit, and I started to sense the buck was being passively handed from one rep to the next as if I were lice. "This sounds like such an amazing idea!" my agent would say. "You know who I'd like you to meet in our talent department who could really help? Brad." Then Brad would say, "This is such a brilliant idea. You know who I'd like you to meet in our lit department who could really help? Britney." Then Britney would say, "This is such a superb concept. You know who I'd like you to meet in our financing department who could really help? Mark." Then Mark would be excited to introduce me to Heather, and Heather would be excited to introduce me to Jan, then Josh, then Bob, then the valet attendant, and so on, until I had virtually disappeared amid the quick passing along of lukewarm hands.

I realized I would have to stop going the traditional route of movie-making and reach Ms. Fitch by my own volition. I noticed that she had given a glowing quote for my friend Derrick C. Brown's new poetry book and asked him if he would consider reaching out on my behalf. He did. A week later, I was having drinks with Janet in a small tiki-themed bar on Sunset Boulevard in Los Angeles. She was still reticent to give me the rights, but she did give me a mailing address so I could send her a copy of my grandfather's violin recordings—like me, she was a big fan of classical music. Soon I had her email address and was checking in and writing her letters almost every week. Eventually, she gave in and offered me the rights to her book.

My writing partner, Ed Dougherty, and I spent a year putting together a solid screenplay based on Janet's novel, but I once again found myself cemented in noes when we began to look for financing for the film. Every financier I met with wondered why a story about a young man who takes his own life is barely a character in the movie. He's in the book, they'd say, so why isn't he in the script? I would explain that the delicate psychological thriller I wanted to make was not about the boy, but about the two women he was leaving behind, his mother and his girlfriend. It would be the absence of the boy that would make the film stronger, I argued, because it would reflect the absence that the women felt. With the boy in the film, it would become a story about a suicide; without him, it would be a story about how the mind fills in the painful blanks of a life once it's gone.

They scratched their heads and one by one passed on the basis that the audience was going to need to see more of the boy in order to make the twisted, grief-stricken relationship between the mother and the girlfriend "more believable," as one investor put it to me over coffee. In fact, more often than not, I routinely heard this exact sentiment from men who were film financiers: this notion that women's grief just didn't make sense without a man being the literal visual center of it. (What a metaphor for real life.) I argued that grief is subjective and mourning is a mercurial journey and that if I conveyed those things with style, uniqueness, and truth, it wouldn't matter who or what the two women were grieving over—it could be a potted plant—the audience would still buy in, because they would be invested not in the past with the boy, but in the future between these two women. The investor slurped his coffee and said, "Sorry. I just don't see it."

Most men in positions of power don't "see it" because they are part of a system that makes it easy for them not to have to look. They see what they were taught to see: a world that advances the stories, careers, sexuality, and intellect of predominantly white men in order to ensure their longevity. If you don't believe me, look at the women in your life and ask yourself if they've been treated unfairly. Is your wife being paid what she is worth? Is your daughter getting the same treatment at school from teachers as your son? Does your partner or girlfriend ever come home and tell you a story about having to deal with an unwanted advance from a coworker? Have you ever watched a female peer have her idea stolen or repurposed by a male superior right in front of you, as if it's par for the course? Have you ever heard any woman say these words: "I have to work twice as hard as a man does"?

I had spent so much of my career and creative life asking for nothing more than to get in the room where projects were being discussed and decisions were being made. I just wanted what I felt so many peers who are men always had: the opportunity, at the very least, to fail. But from where I and so many other women like me have stood, we don't even have the opportunity to get in the room to make our case. This is especially true for women who are not white and cis.

Investing in movies directed by women, about women, for women is considered a big risk. Our stories are not seen as equal in power or potential success because most men want to see versions of themselves in the films they are financing. But here's the thing: so do women. So do nonbinary people. We have entire interior lives that do not include thoughts on or about men. At all. (Shocking, I know!) Meanwhile, 60 percent of moviegoing audiences are made up of women and two of the largest blockbusters in the last decade—*Twilight* and *A Wrinkle in Time*—were both directed by women. And yet only 7 percent of directors in the film industry annually are women and a fraction of that are non-white women. Why?

I decided that if I was ever going to get my movie

made, I was going to have to stop trying to get my foot in the door where men were making creative decisions and instead just build my own goddamn house.

Janet Fitch was the first woman to believe in my creative capability and give me an opportunity during this time. Before I could write a script or shoot the film based on that script, I had to convince her to give me the rights to her book. She was extremely hesitant at first, and rightfully so. All she knew of me was that I was an actress in love with her novel. (Get in line!) But the difference between Janet Fitch and most men to whom I have worked hard to prove myself is that after doing the work to convince her I was the right woman for job—after earning the right to be considered at all—she actually saw what I was capable of and said yes. This is the hurdle that most women like myself can never seem to get over and what sets my experience with Janet apart from the other experiences I've had of trying to win the job. If I did get in a room to be considered, I was chosen rarely, if ever. And I'm not just talking about the rejection of auditioning; I'm talking about the rejection of vision, of perspective, and of creative choice; the rejection of power.

There have been so many instances in rooms practically devoid of female representation where I've pitched an idea to men and the answer on the other side of the table was always: "It's certainly an interesting idea but we don't see it working." First the compliment, followed by the backhand. Time and time again I've heard men say that something I've created or thought of was fresh or unique or even bold, only to have them reject it anyway. Men are happy to have me give them notes or rework their scripts—for free, of course—and then incorporate my feedback with fervor only to cast a different actress in the lead role.

Why is it that most men in positions to make choices rarely choose works by women? And if they do, why do they see it as a risk? As taking a chance? Isn't that all of filmmaking? Some combination of knowledge, luck, and risk? You could have a great film on your hands and pour millions of dollars into its marketing and still come out with a dud at the box office. It happens every single week. It is *all* risk. So why not hire women and produce our stories—stories that inject life into a white, male-centered, oversaturated art form with narratives that the public is frankly bored of watching? What stops men from seeing the choices of women as something inspired instead of unsure?

There are many answers to these questions, but the simplest just might be that there is a deep, subconscious fear of being replaced, of having their voices end up like our own: marginalized. That might seem like a leap, but for the most part, men naturally gravitate toward stories that represent their own experiences as a way of making sure they don't disappear from the cultural narrative. Their taste in television, filmmaking, and literature is often blatantly slanted toward creating worlds and characters and narratives that look and sound like their own. It's part of their form of survival to protect the lens through which our culture has always seen the male gaze.

Even women characters that are written by men end up sounding more like men—like a sixteen-year-old Jonathan Franzen fantasy rather than an actual woman. Women, on the other hand, rarely have this problem in reverse. Perhaps because we have grown up so deeply entrenched in the psyches of men and their stories that we've become virtual scholars on their subject matter, extremely knowledgeable on their point of view. Repetitive stories of wars, espionage, parties in Vegas, or a game of tag. (That exists, by the way . . . a whole movie about guys playing tag. It took me all of two seconds to guess that the film was written and directed by white men.)

Unlike many of these men who are able to give green lights but instead opt for red ones when it comes to female filmmakers, Janet Fitch was completely different. Ms. Fitch has a nose for bullshit—especially women's bullshit—which is one of the reasons why it's not just her female protagonists that are so compelling, but her female antagonists too. She got me because she gets women. And after I spent a few months sending her letters and showing her my vision for the film—after she saw that I was more than just an actress, but also a poet, and the granddaughter of a concert master violinist, and the great-granddaughter of a Daughter of the American Revolution—she knew that if she was going to take a chance on anything, it should be taking a chance on me.

After writing the script for *Paint It Black*, I spent almost a year working on the material with director Courtney Hunt. After some time it became clear that we had very different creative visions for the film. Hers was gritty, a raucous catfight. My vision was stylized, crisp, and intentional; imagine David Lynch directing *Grey Gardens*. After many creative discussions, Courtney finally told me she didn't feel like she should be the one to direct anymore. Because I should.

While this moment was akin to handing me a grenade full of freedom, I still needed someone to push me to rip out the pin. That person was the other producer of the film, Wren Arthur. After Courtney and I parted ways, Wren called me on the phone to discuss the idea of my directing. I balked at the notion, saying I had no real experience. "Don't you, though?" she asked me. Despite all the frustration and outspokenness I had vocalized about there not being enough opportunities for women, here was one clearly presenting itself to me, and yet my immediate reaction was still one of self-doubt.

Did I have enough experience, I wondered? I kind

of did. I had been an actress for more than two decades and had worked with some of the best and some of the worst directors. But out of all the directors of television and feature films in those two decades, so very few were women. In all the feature films I have ever appeared in, only four were directed by women. And in the hundreds of episodes of television I have done over the years, I can count on one hand the women directors I've worked with. Until the TV pilot I shot last year for FX, *Y: The Last Man,* only once in my entire twenty-five-year career in television or feature films had I worked with a black woman director, and never had I worked with a black woman showrunner. I've never even acted in a starring role alongside a black woman costar.

On sets throughout my career, I watched how directors brought their visions to fruition; I got to see firsthand the mistakes, the brilliant ideas, the stress of losing the light, and the value of a really good first assistant director. On top of that, I had spent years mastering the delicate art of suggesting ideas to male directors in a way that didn't undermine their vision but, rather, strengthened it. I also spent over a decade giving copious amounts of notes on screenplays or pilots anytime a male writer would ask, strengthening their female protagonists and helping them see the sharper version of what they were trying to convey in a woman's voice. And in the process I was learning the ropes of writing and directing by simply participating. Many women don't count this as enough experience but it absolutely is. And yet I still found myself sitting there, as if across the table from a young Hillary Clinton in Arkansas, saying to myself: *Are you sure?*

But I knew this would be one of my greatest opportunities and something that could change the course of my entire life. I knew I could learn on the job if there were things I didn't know how to do already, because I had (ironically) learned to do that from watching men do it my entire life. I just had to find the guts to start by saying yes.

And so I did. I told Wren I wanted to direct my own film.

What came next was a kind of support I'd never experienced before in my career. Wren sat me down and said, "Now listen to me, a lot of people are going to try and convince us that you shouldn't be doing this. That we should pick someone with more experience. Fuck them. You are going to be brilliant. You have a vision and I believe in it wholeheartedly." Wren's unwavering belief in me was an example of the power of being professional allies and mentors to each other in a business whose business it is to marginalize women's narratives, both behind the camera and in front of it.

One of the most important gifts we can give one another, regardless of gender, is the gift of not only being believed but being believed in. It never ceases to amaze me how even the smallest gesture of support can be life changing for those who have spent years being told their ideas don't matter. Recently I did an interview with the writer and cultural critic Rebecca Carroll for WNYC radio in which we talked about the business of allyship between different kinds of women, and the importance of not just talking about it but living it. I have taken much for granted with regard to the reach I have been afforded through my career and have not fully considered what I have to offer, no matter how limited my own personal power within the industry might be. I have used the excuse of comparing myself to hugely influential actors and directors as a way of telling myself and others that it's harder for me to support someone who is not in the entertainment business because I do not have the same power that others do. But what I've come to realize is that it's not about my level of fame, it's about my level of *access*, and that is something I have plenty of.

I told Rebecca that in the last year part of my own personal Era of Ignition has been to harvest the power I *do* have, regardless of how little I feel it might be, to open a door for someone who has never had the same opportunities as I did. For instance, most industry people I know hate going to award show after-parties, myself included, even though we get invited to them all the time. Many actors go to these events only if they are nominated, presenting, or have an active TV show or film with the company that is throwing the party. But what about some young aspiring writer or person fresh out of film school who would love nothing more than the opportunity to rub shoulders with the likes of Ted Sarandos, chief content officer for Netflix, or get the chance to introduce themselves and their work to the likes of TV show creator and powerhouse Jenji Kohan? Whenever I'm invited to these parties now, I try to bring with me someone who might benefit from such an evening. Rebecca nodded her head and said, "I must tell you, I would've given anything to have someone in my corner like that when I was first starting out."

Being in one another's corners is an effective and simple way for people to both support each other and also feel supported, and we don't do enough of it. No matter what industry you're in, consider what you have access to that others may not and offer your assistance. If you are of cis gender, consider how a nonbinary or trans person could feel supported and seen by you. If you are a white woman, consider how nonwhite women could be supported and seen by you.

Being allies willing to use our access in support of others applies to services like health care and nonprofit organizations, too. Until the Affordable Care Act, among other discriminatory practices, it was completely legal to deny necessary health care to transgender people, including transition-related care. Similarly, the Black Lives Matter movement was created to bring awareness of the unjust murders of black people in communities whose livelihoods are so threatened that they can't even protest their own neighbors' murders peacefully without succumbing to physical harm at the hands of police and racists (who are sometimes one and the same) or, in the case of Colin Kaepernick, being blacklisted by the NFL and losing his entire career for taking a knee during the national anthem in support of such protests. Simply showing up and fighting for equality regardless of your race or class—simply being in the corner of those who are disenfranchised when the world is not—you will make a difference.

It is also important not to forget to be allies to ourselves. Deciding that I would direct my own film was an act of solidarity toward my own fulfillment, the kind of gift I had rarely been afforded, or afforded myself, throughout my career. The very act of saying yes to directing opened a door in my mind—a door I always knew was there but assumed was locked and closed off to me—and when I walked through it, I was no longer afraid of what I would find.

After saying yes to myself, to my own potential, I thought of all the years I had spent waiting to hear the no I knew was inevitably coming from a representative or producer after any given meeting or job interview. And by waiting for it, by expecting it, by knowing it was the rule, I had done myself a great disservice in not listening to my most vital instinct and pursuing my goals at all costs. I remembered all the times I had been told to manage my expectations, or to consider alternatives, or to accept the fact that there weren't a lot of options for women like me outside of acting and to just be grateful for what I had. When I said yes to directing my movie, I was freed of that myth, regardless of whether or not the film succeeded. Because the success had already taken place. The success was in saying yes.

4

On the first day of pre-production for the shoot of *Paint It Black,* I sat down at a production meeting with the heads of all the different departments who would be working on our film—the director of photography, the costume designer, the production designer, the hair and makeup team, and many more. As I entered the room and sat down in my chair, everyone opened their notebooks and looked at me with smiles on their faces and excitement to begin our work together. I too smiled and opened my notebook, waiting for someone in charge to initiate the meeting. Then, in a split second, I realized: The person in charge was me. For the first time in my entire career, people were looking to me, and me alone, for answers.

I instantly flushed with emotions, equal parts

thrilled and petrified. *So this is what it feels like to be your own creative engineer,* I thought. What an intoxicating feeling—to be the one calling the shots in the room, the very kind of room I had been kept out of for years. It was bittersweet to say the least. I collected myself and opened my director's book and looked over to my creative partner in the making of the film, Brian Rigney Hubbard, a seasoned and visionary director of photography. He looked at me and nodded as if to say, *you got this.*

Working alongside this phenomenal team of gifted people, we collaborated on everything from establishing the right tone for the film, to selecting color palettes for characters' clothing, to deciding what kind of furniture each character would have in their house. Alongside the DP Brian, the production designer Markus Kirschner, the costume designer Christine Peters, the other two brilliant producers, Amy Hobby and Anne Hubbell, and the entire hardworking crew, I was able to create the type of film I had always dreamed my screenplay would become: a film slightly arch in tone with a deeply satisfying emotional underpinning to drive the psychodrama of the plot and the magnetism between two starkly different women drawn together by circumstance, brilliantly played by Alia Shawkat and Janet McTeer.

With my background in storytelling as both an actress and a poet, directing felt natural to me, perhaps because I had grown up around it and was privy to seeing all the ways in which directors succeed, but also fail. I've watched as directors executed brilliant, tricky camera shots while other directors wasted much of their shooting time on multiple shots, adjusting some flower vase deep in the background that bugged them but that no audience member would ever think twice about. But even with the privilege of getting that behind-the-scenes experience from such a young age, something ignited in me the first time I ever called "Action." Something that went beyond the teachable and touched on the preternatural—something primal. During one particularly tough shooting day that involved the use of a jib crane (where the camera is mounted on a large weighted crane so it can move to much higher angles), we had to stage a fight scene in which McTeer chokes Shawkat's character over her son's casket at his funeral. Shawkat then falls to the ground and scampers up the aisle among mourners' chairs, as McTeer drops to her knees and starts pulling the carpet toward her, as if pulling this poor innocent girl toward her doom, like some giant tongue of a monster about to swallow her whole. The scene had to run a very careful and extremely balanced line between being utterly terrifying and being so horrendous that the audience almost laughs out of sheer horror from the spectacle of it. I had prepared a series of shots from different angles: I planned an aerial shot, a shot from the hallway, and one from the point of view of McTeer, bringing Shawkat closer one pull at a time.

The jib had been an expensive item in our film's budget and required several hours of assembly, and I had a long shot list for the scenes I wanted to shoot that day. As the day progressed, it was becoming clear that we were not going to make our day if we did not cut many of the shots I had planned to do. The producers felt we should cut the rug-pull shots and use the jib as much as possible; even Brian agreed, concerned that while those angles would be great, they may not be worth the risk of sacrificing the use of the jib and the other shots we had planned. But my gut was telling me something more important: If I could capture the ferociousness of McTeer's character in this specific way, with this specific sequence—of her dragging a young girl down an aisle at a funeral—then no other shot would matter, not even an expensive aerial crane shot. I went with my gut. I pulled the jib for the remainder of the day, and Brian and I proceeded with the rug-pulling shots.

Later, when the film debuted at Film Independent's LA Film Festival, that particular moment during the funeral scene was one of the most talked about and gravitated toward scenes, by audiences and film critics alike. Peter Travers from *Rolling Stone* said, "It's impossible to quantify what it takes to be a quality director—but damn, you know it when you see it. And you'll see it clear and strong in *Paint*

45

It Black, a staggeringly impressive feature directing debut for actress Amber Tamblyn." Of the rug-
pulling scene, Travers wrote, "[Meredith and Josie's]
confrontation at the young man's funeral is not
something you'll soon forget."

When all was said and done, the risk I had taken
in believing in that choice—my own instinct—paid
off. The experience of making difficult yet informed
instinctual decisions that actually were worth it in
the long run changed me forever. I could get rejected
for jobs in acting, directing, or writing for the rest
of my life, but nothing would ever take away what
the experience of directing my first feature film had
taught me: that I know myself better than I think I
do and that I know my worth better than others think
they do.

While I was ultimately able to leverage my tenure
in the entertainment business—*and* find a benefac-
tor to invest in my movie through her strong belief in
me as a filmmaker—not every woman gets this kind
of opportunity. So how do we harness this long-
silenced instinct of ours into daily creative life without having to leverage everything we have in order
to make it happen? Part of the answer lies in not just
thinking outside of the box, but working to re-create
it altogether. Consider the filmmaker Sean Baker,
whose film *Tangerine,* about a transgender sex worker,
was shot on just three iPhones with a total budget of $100,000. The film debuted at the Sundance

Film Festival and garnered much critical acclaim. Choosing to film his movie in this way sent a message to so many aspiring filmmakers and artists that you can, in fact, make a movie that is relatively cost-effective and inspired; you just have to think about how to do it differently. And yes, *Tangerine* grossed a million dollars at the box office and changed the way many people perceived their ability to get a movie made. Baker also made a powerful statement by choosing to make a story about trans people that actually cast trans actors in those roles. At the time, this was, sadly, a revolutionary idea, especially coming from a cis white male filmmaker. In an interview with *The Wrap*, Baker said of the two lead actresses, "My hope is that people recognize their great talent so they can parlay this into their dreams and their futures. . . . Now that more trans roles are being written, it's time to look at trans actors who can play these roles." I couldn't agree more. Widening the scope of what and who we see on screens only enriches our world and cultural points of view.

Women have always struggled to take creative power into our own hands—a power that has traditionally been denied to us or, perversely, has been lent to us for a time, before we have to give it back to the rightful owners. From the powers of our bodies, to the power of political office, to the power of our public oratory voice, to our creative power. All of these struggles with gaining power are particularly difficult battles that women face because there is a chance we will not succeed in our endeavor, and more often than not we don't get second chances to try and succeed again in the same ways that men do. Because women have to work twice as hard to prove themselves and their value the first time, a second chance for a woman with a lot of potential is often seen as a bad gamble, whereas a second chance for a man with a lot of potential is usually seen as a good investment. We are told by the world around us that we will not succeed unless we proceed in a manner that is pleasing, creatively and otherwise, to those in positions of authority.

But I challenge that notion and believe each of us has the ability to help expand the way we see art, and to expand even further the voices that get to participate in that art. As the artist Georgia O'Keefe once said, "To create one's own world takes courage." And it also takes community. We must continue to build communities of people who believe in one another and work to create spaces for more art to exist. We must continue to fight not just for the brilliant and already powerful women who are out there in the world making waves, but also for those who are still failing, and are willing to keep failing until they succeed, if ever. Because it will be the normalizing of women's potential that will not just bring about the way we value work by women, but also shine a much-needed light on the ways in which we have been taught to value, period.

Bottom line: Until women are allowed to make mediocre works of art while still succeeding in the way that many white men get to do this every single day, we will not have the power to take our creative freedoms back. We will be limited by impossible expectations reserved for the few. As long as we are put and put ourselves on a patriarchal pedestal, too high to succeed and doomed to fail, then surely we will be set up to do exactly that, every time.

5

My experience directing and taking back creative control was life altering, but the battle was far from over. The film had been rejected by one of the most important film festivals in the world. The reason given by one of the festival directors was they felt they had already filled the slot in their lineup for an actress-turned-director. (This would never be said to an actor-turned-director.) And even later, when the film garnered strong reviews and audience praise, the movie had a nearly impossible journey being sold, despite a score of 96 percent on Rotten Tomatoes at the time and glowing reviews. Who are these gatekeepers, I wondered, deciding what women's work gets seen and what doesn't, what succeeds and what doesn't?

After the festival experience, the film was then rejected by a well-known indie film distribution company, despite having a triple-threat pedigree: a multi-Academy-Award-nominated actress in Janet McTeer and a young rising star in Alia Shawkat, both of whom received phenomenally strong reviews, and a fresh female filmmaker who could pull double the publicity weight by being a veteran actress and the youngest director they'd ever acquired a film from. I was at my wits' end, equal parts frustrated, confused, and just plain pissed off about the company's rejection of our film. I decided that "we are passing" was not an acceptable answer and hired a statistician to analyze the more than 420 films made since this company's inception. I planned on giving the report to the three male executives who ran the studio, along with the submission of my film a second time.

We found that 36 of the 420 films were written and directed by women, roughly 8 percent of the total releases. The number of films written and directed by men was 245, roughly 57 percent of the total releases. In total, 378 out of 420 films were directed by men. I also pointed out that the company had a history of putting out the debut films of male actors-turned-directors. We found that the currency and marketability of these actors were likely part of the reason these films were bought in the first place, and then we proceeded to give statistics as to why my film would do the same. I spoke about the press opportunities I could bring to the film as well as the public figures who had pledged to amplify the promotion of the film. The statistician and I made a spreadsheet that broke down every single one of the company's movies into categories based on how much they cost to make, which ones got into which film festivals, what their scores were on Rotten Tomatoes, what they grossed at the box office, whether they were directed by a woman or a man, and the age of those men and women at the time they had directed their films. In the report's closing I wrote this:

"Finally, let me ask you this question: With the relationships I have presented, the film I've made, and the extremely strong reviews the film received, if this movie had been written and directed by a man in his fifties, would you have bought it? Based on all the debut films by male writers/directors you've acquired, and the male creative careers you've shepherded along the way, and the culmination of reviews, and the festivals to which they were accepted (including those by first-time actors-turned-directors), the answer is yes. Yes, you would've bought this film if I were a man."

The three men who run this distribution company responded by saying how impressed they were by the report, and then they turned me down a second time.

PAINT IT BLACK eventually did find a good dis-
tributor in Imagination Worldwide, a small company
owned by a woman. The movie would make its way
into theaters for a limited run and, eventually, onto
Netflix. I was forever a changed woman, unable to
un-know what I had come to understand about my
own aptitude and potential throughout the process,
regardless of who turned me down. An ember was
igniting, a flame most needed and new. I felt different. Capable. Potent. The invisible alphabet was
revealing new letters, bridging me toward my future.

On the night of the film's premiere in Los Angeles, I found myself exhausted in a way I had never
experienced before. I told myself it was nerves. Before the movie started I had plans to get my hair and
makeup done at my hairstylist's house. Since I was
coming straight from a long day of press for the film,
I couldn't drive all the way back across town to my
house and make it back in time for the premiere. So
I asked my hairstylist, Creighton, if I could come kill
some time at his house before we were to start the
glamming process. I lay down on his guest bed and
fell asleep for over two hours.

After the premiere that night, I caught a ride in
Quentin Tarantino's car over to the after-party at a

nearby restaurant. He couldn't stop talking about how much he loved the film and I couldn't stop thinking about lying down for a nap. I discreetly put the passenger-side seat back just a little so I could close my eyes while he rambled on ecstatically about camera shots and angles and questions about camera filters and lenses. "Mmm hmmm" was all I could muster in response.

Later in the evening my sister texted me to say she looked at pictures from the red carpet and wondered if I was pregnant. "Why do you say that?" I asked. "Your face," she began, "you've let go of something to make space for something else. I can see it in your face."

The next morning, I had just put most of the dishes and cups in the dishwasher when I decided to get on with it and take the pregnancy test I had bought but hadn't yet found the courage to take. *Fuck it,* I thought—*let's do this.* I grabbed a shot glass I had bought on a trip to Hawaii that read SOMETHING MAGICAL HAPPENS HERE!, peed into it, and dropped the white pregnancy stick strip into the glass. I sat and waited as the two-minute countdown began and an answer awaited me on the counter. When the stick finished processing and the result came in, I texted my sister back: "You asshole. You always have to be right, don't you?"

6

After two of the longest and most difficult passion projects I had ever worked on had finally come to fruition, *Dark Sparkler*, which had taken six years to write and sell, and *Paint It Black*, I braced myself for that old familiar feeling of pure dread—of not being ready to be a mother yet. But unlike the last time I found myself in this situation, my first feeling was one of immediate joy. I was, of course, still extremely terrified, but it was different this time. Before, I had started sinking immediately, drifting away from myself, thinking of ways I could disappear from this new, unwanted trajectory. But this time I felt strong, competent—I felt ready.

David was traveling in Europe on a stand-up tour at the time and I was about to join him in London. I decided to tell him the good news when I got there, instead of over the phone. I carried the pregnancy test in my backpack all the way to the UK and my big plan was to reveal the news to him by replacing his toothbrush with the pregnancy test one night before bed. (I didn't end up following through with that plan. Instead, I dropped the positive pregnancy test in an envelope and mailed it to a famously anti-choice, anti-woman senator with a note that read, "Tag, you're it!" just for shits and giggles.)

I'll keep the moment I told David he was going to become a father just between us, because it's a most sacred moment to me, and one I will forever cherish for the rest of my life. It lives alongside some of the best and worst things we've been through in our eleven years together. But what I can tell you is, he cried a little. Yes, David Cross shed actual tears.

We were overjoyed with the hope of becoming new parents, and I could not believe my unimaginable luck: I would be bringing a child into the world the same year of the election of the first female president of the United States, Hillary Rodham Clinton. And not just any child—a girl.

My history with Mrs. Clinton goes back far before her 2008 and 2016 bids for the presidency. I met her in 2003 when I was twenty years old and working on the TV show *Joan of Arcadia*. Mary Steenburgen played my mother and had been a very close friend of Mrs. Clinton for a long time. I would go see Hillary speak publicly, often off the cuff, when I always found her to be the strongest version of her public-speaking self. She was an instant inspiration for me because I had never seen anyone like her before, a woman who paved a path right up to the very top of the political system, no matter the hurdles along the way.

Hillary was the reason I signed up to work at voting locations and volunteered for Heal the Bay and began working closely with organizations like Planned Parenthood. I would speak on behalf of affordable health care for women to members of the Senate and the House, arguing that access to affordable birth control went beyond just contraception, it was also used to treat chronic illnesses like endometriosis. I began my activism through my writing and poetry as a teenager, but I began my physical activism after I met Hillary Clinton in my early twenties.

When Hillary announced her candidacy for the first time, in 2008, I was twenty-five and completely ecstatic. I quickly reached out to her campaign to support it in any way that I could, and soon I was working closely with her and her daughter, Chelsea, as part of the campaign's youth outreach program, alongside my best friend and fellow Hillary cheerleader, America Ferrera. We traveled with her, speaking at rallies and events in more than twenty states over the course of the year.

Once, while boarding Hillary's campaign plane, America and I looked for seats together on the large

757, and Hillary's assistant Huma Abedin called out to us, "Ladies, we have two seats for you up here." We followed her up to the front of the plane, and Hillary pointed to the two seats directly behind her and smiled. As the plane took off, America and I peeked through the crack between the seats in front of us and watched as she pulled out a thick stack of papers in preparation for the debate that was happening that evening with then-Senator Barack Obama. Hillary took out a legal pad and leafed through papers covered with copious amounts of notes and a few Post-its. She remained working like that, without breaking, for close to four hours, until the sun started to dip outside the plane's windows and she needed to turn on an overhead light to keep going. America had fallen asleep next to me and my eyes grew heavy too with the lull of the plane. Before I fell asleep, I watched Hillary turn a stapled page and stick a Post-it note onto it that read, "This is very important."

That night's debate marked the beginning of a decade-long narrative about women in power and perfectionism, one that was not new but clearly not disappearing anytime soon. Mr. Obama chuckled onstage, crossed his legs, and flippantly told Mrs. Clinton, "Don't worry, Hillary, you're likable enough." I'm sure he meant no harm with the comment, but it stirred up many negative feelings for women like me across America: that we had to be likable, agreeable, and enjoyable in order to have any say in this country. She herself had made some equally tone-deaf jabs at the senator during the course of the campaign, but I'm highlighting this particular statement because it struck a chord that still rings out today. Most women are used to being told how unlikable we are, in a variety of coded ways—of how disagreeable, irrational, or even repellent we act, speak, or think. What I didn't know then was that the importance of Hillary's physical, emotional, and superficial appeal would carry itself well into her next presidential run and even deeper into the zeitgeist of America's noxious history with all of womankind.

I began to collect unsettling Hillary Clinton dolls and memorabilia along my campaign travels, which could be found in gas stations and retail shops across the country. One was a Hillary nutcracker that showed her arms folded in a blue suit with zigzagged blades running up her inner thighs. Another was an unflattering singing replica that squealed, "When my husband lied, I stood right by his side, now it's my time to shine, let freedom reign." Most people would call these things merchandise. But to me they were dark artifacts, proof of our poisonous conclusions about women who dare to be ambitious. I collected cartoons and drawings from magazines and newspapers of Hillary as a devil with horns and a tail that stabbed men, or Hillary as a screaming, obese nag, or Hillary turning a blind eye to her husband Bill's wandering one. Hillary the shrew. Cackling Hillary the war-thirsty. Hillary the torturer. The fake mother. The secret lesbian. The Wall Street shill. The "monster," as self-described feminist Samantha Power once called her. I collected an entire scrapbook of these forms of sexism in articles, newspapers, and interviews. Someday it would just be a relic, I told myself, remnants of America's antiquated hatred toward us. Little did I know, some of the most feral rhetoric against women was yet to come.

I entered into that first campaign in 2008 activated and without weariness, eager to be a part of something big and meaningful. But when Hillary lost the primary to the more likable man with very little governing experience, it felt like something different from politics as usual. It felt like patriarchy as usual. It wasn't about losing to a man, it was about a system that enables men to regularly win over women, across industries, job titles, and careers.

In June 2008, after the primary was over and Hillary had lost, *New York* magazine put her on its cover and called her a "superstar," stating that she wouldn't be president but she would become something "far more interesting." The media in that moment had finally decided to give her permission to be seen as likable, an underhanded compliment for her mark on history. I cut out that magazine cover and taped it to my desk, where it remained for six years. Over her mouth I placed a Post-it note that read, "This is very important."

I stared at her face every day during my volatile twenties; I stared at her when I came undone, when nothing felt fair, when everything seemed out of reach, out of my hands, and out of gas. She was there when the fire of my life was fuming, and still there when the flames died down to a lean gleaming. When I ignited and when I extinguished. All the while, her steady half-smile looked up at me, unwavering.

7

Years after I stared at the defeated face of Hillary Clinton on the cover of that magazine back in 2008, I found myself once again preparing for the polarization and pain I knew was coming the moment she announced a second candidacy in the spring of 2015. A video debuted on the *New York Times* website and I instantly felt a knot tighten in my stomach. "I'm getting ready to do something, too," the voice in the video declared. The first half showcased diverse stories from people across America, talking about things they were getting ready for: childbirth, retirement, opening a new business. The camera cut to the back of a woman talking to a man in a deli. The man smiled as he looked at her and I paused the video to study him—his Yankees cap and gray hoodie tucked inside a black jacket, his laugh, his sincere pleasure in whatever it was the woman was saying. Two men stood behind him, also watching her, intrigued. Engaged.

I didn't want the moment to end, so I left the video paused on my computer for days. I would go back to the image frequently and study his frozen happy face and the woman's head, frozen in mid nod. The moment was picturesque, a surreal dream from which I never wanted to wake up. *Men love this powerful woman. Men are not threatened by this woman. Men find warmth, kindness, and strength in this woman. Men take what she has to say seriously. Men do not talk over her but, instead, listen. Men see her as their emotional and intellectual equal.* Which in turn could also mean: Men love powerful women. Men are not threatened by women. Men find warmth, kindness, and strength in women. Men take what we have to say seriously. Men do not talk over us but, instead, listen. Men see us as their emotional and intellectual equals.

The video had been released four days earlier and I felt like the only person in the western hemisphere who hadn't watched it yet. I hadn't watched it because I wasn't ready to. When I looked at the paused image of the man's engaged face, I could live in a world where this woman was not the bull's-eye on the target of American misogyny. But I knew when I saw her face in the next frame I'd be forced to feel everything that had been projected onto her presence. I took a deep breath and pressed "play."

"I'm running for president," Hillary Clinton said, as the camera cut to her confident, beaming smile.

I had been through the excruciating experience of this woman running for office once before and I didn't know if I could go through it again. It took me almost an entire year to fully get behind her as a candidate—not because I didn't want to, but because I was afraid to. I was afraid she would lose again. And I couldn't bear that loss and everything that would come with it a second time.

But when I found out I was pregnant a year after that video debuted, in the summer of 2016, I felt an obligation to put my fears aside and support her. Hillary Clinton didn't need my endorsement, but *I* needed it. Now with a child inside me, a little girl, I had to be brave. What if that was my daughter in a video like that some day? Wouldn't I feel extremely polarized emotions? A mix of protection and fear and pride? Wouldn't it be easier to just cheer Mrs. Clinton on from the sidelines this time instead of putting myself out there and traveling around the country listening to all the ways in which Americans mythologized her into some monster?

I know it doesn't seem like that big of a deal to publicly endorse a candidate, but this went so much deeper than the narrative of politics as usual. This was unusual politics: a woman, wholly capable and qualified, going for a second chance after viciously losing the first time. I had to find strength and resolve in knowing I was going to have to watch her get attacked unfairly, and be attacked myself for supporting her. It was going to get ugly. Really ugly.

I tried to explain my hesitancy to David. I told him how I felt, that I couldn't take the rejection of Mrs. Clinton again, that there was too much at stake for my future desires and hopes for our unborn daughter. That it all added up, and it was absolutely all connected. David, like many well-meaning guys I know, would say, "Don't worry, honey. When Marlow grows up she can be anything she puts her mind to." To which I would say, "That's just it, though. She can't. It's literally been proven that women can't."

These types of formulaic sentiments, while well intentioned, have always frustrated me. They feel more like an easy aspirational quote rather than the harder truth: things have yet to change for women and what we are allowed or not allowed to put our minds to. Putting our minds to something has never been the problem. The problem has been: Who decides whose mind is worthy? We like to hope for the best for our daughters, telling them to follow their dreams and anything can come true, but often this is just not the case. I know we mean well, but it's hard for me to stomach when the intentions of those sentiments just don't match the reality of the world in which our daughters are growing up. Same goes for our daughters and their sexual safety. It is terrifying, as a mother, to think about what my daughter could someday be put through behind a closed door, only to have her tell her story and end up being character-assassinated and completely disbelieved, the way so many women are.

How do we encourage and support our daughters by talking to them and making them feel powerful without lying to them about the realities of the world we live in? How do we not simply tell them they can be anything they put their minds to, but help shape those minds, and the minds of people in positions of power, so that our daughters have a better chance of that becoming true? I also think about the conversations black mothers have to have with their daughters and how those conversations might differ from my own.

I spoke to my friend Mahogany L. Browne, who recently taught a course at Pratt Institute called "Space & Power: The Black Woman Body as an American Technology," which looks at the ways in which the black female body has been used as a machine to churn out cultural phenomena in art. I asked her about the conversations she, as a black mother, has had to have with her daughter, especially conversations pertaining to consent and sexual awareness. "I've been super vigilant about my daughter's right to say no and what spaces and conditions are around us that make us think we are obligated to say yes to someone," she told me over the phone recently. "No one gets to tell my daughter how the barometer reads as far as when and if she gets to say no—whether you're kissing someone or not. She is the only barometer for yes or no. No one else. And this is the hardest thing for me to talk to her about because I'm not sure I even believe it myself—the reality of it. Because this idea of chosen consent for our daughters is the way it's supposed to be in utopia, but this isn't utopia. This is the real world."

I asked her about how race plays a part in these conversations with her daughter and if that's something that comes up more frequently than not. "Look," she said, "making consent possible for a young black girl in this country is literally a magic trick. Every black mother has to pull faith out of a hat and pray it's not revealed to be something else instead. We have such a hard time believing we even have a voice to begin with, as black girls and women. And while I talk to her about sexual assault and consent as a woman, her race is always the container of that and any conversation. It is the container that holds everything we do, say, are subjected to, and live by. Because we are living in a world where people don't just see women as women, they see the color of our skin *first,* and that comes with a lot of inherent, ingrained feelings. So they are allowed to treat me a certain way. I tell my daughter that as black women we will always be asked to worry about the woman part, but never about the other part—the color of our skin part. Forget about that part, people will say to you, that part doesn't matter as much."

This container Browne refers to is something white mothers will never have to take into consideration when protecting their children, which is why white apathy—most especially white liberal apathy— during an election cycle is one of the most selfish acts of privilege in which we participate. To say you are willing to sit out an election because a candidate does not tick every single one of your boxes is a form of self-centered blindness. Consider the children of minority families—of minority women—who have everything to lose from someone like Donald Trump becoming president, while the rest of us merely have everything to choose from.

I WAS FINISHING UP my first trimester of pregnancy when I saw Hillary on television one evening doing an interview. In it, she said something about the world we would be handing over to our children and wasn't it worth fighting for. I thought about the daughter I was carrying inside me. About Mahogany's daughter. And about all the sons of the mothers I love, too; the responsibility and accountability they would someday carry, with their own futures as men, especially with regard to our daughters. I knew

then that it didn't matter how I felt or what I needed—
my fear, my uncertainty, my agitation, my election
PTSD—this was about a future that didn't belong to
me; it belongs to our children—*all* of them.

The very first show of support I made for Hillary's
campaign was a video compilation featuring some of
the strongest and most influential women in entertainment today. Each of us looking into the camera
and simply saying, "I'm with her." I let myself feel
the excitement once again to publicly support this
woman, now a grandmother with even more experience under her belt as secretary of state. I posted
the video on Instagram and Facebook and the comments began to roll in. Suddenly, Hillary being "likable enough" seemed like a compliment compared
to this new level of disparaging language that was
being used to describe her—and me for endorsing
her. "Feel the Bern, you dumb ugly bitch," read one.
"Yet another dumb female I now have to unfollow.
#FeeltheBern." And also, "Lying-ass bitch." There
were well over a hundred comments using demean-
ing language like this. Overall, there was a hostility
in the air unlike anything I had ever felt before—
a foreshadowing of everything vile to come.

When Senator Bernie Sanders entered the presidential race as a candidate in 2015, he sparked a
powerful and important grassroots movement, inspiring millions of people across the country. But he
also sparked something else—something dangerous

and harmful for narratives about women. Along with the enthusiasm that many of Mr. Sanders's supporters brought to his campaign, they also projected a disturbing moral entitlement, bordering on a superiority complex that resulted in verbal cruelty toward anyone who so much as dared to breathe Hillary Clinton's name in their presence or online. Obviously, not every person who supported Mr. Sanders behaved like this, but a lot did, some without even realizing it. Almost every interaction I had with supporters of Mr. Sanders over the course of a full year campaigning for Hillary involved a vitriolic personal attack, whether in person in the dozens of states I visited along the campaign trail, in reaction to my posts on social media, or in response to the op-eds I wrote.

Liberals won't want to hear this, but it's the truth: The deeply misogynist tone that spurred the 2016 election did not begin with Donald Trump. It began with Bernie Sanders and the paramount importance his supporters put on making sure this man succeeded at all costs—costs that included willingly using decades-old lies and sexist smear tactics originated by the Republican party to slowly chip away at Hillary Clinton's dignity and honor as a woman and a mother. I understand the extreme passion that can come with a candidate whom we deeply believe in, but there was an infantile callousness that belied a lot of the passion for Mr. Sanders, paraded out by both men and women who felt as if their progressiveness could only extend to their own beliefs but absolutely not to generations of other liberal women who had longed to see the physical embodiment of progress in a living, breathing, qualified, Democratic woman candidate.

After Hillary had secured the nomination, Bernie Sanders did, eventually, campaign for her in what will forever feel like a feeble gesture of forced solidarity. He clearly felt cheated out of the party's nomination, and everyone could see it. His attitude, a very public sulking, was a striking example of male privilege and the kind of behavior no female candidate could ever get away with had she lost the nomination. In fact, just eight years earlier, Hillary Clinton was the one who had lost, and she got behind then–Democratic nominee Barack Obama with grace and spirit.

I'll never forget the time America Ferrera and I were set to speak just before Mr. Sanders at a rally after Hillary had won the Democratic nomination in 2016. We were waiting backstage and I told Mr. Sanders my husband was a huge supporter and admirer of his and had donated and campaigned on his behalf. "Thank him for me," the senator said. I asked him if we could take a photograph together so I could send it to my husband, but also post it online—an olive branch to bridge the deep divide between our two bases. I didn't want anyone to hate anyone else anymore. I wanted Bernie supporters to get on board with an amazing female candidate, and I wanted Hillary supporters who had been screamed at and talked down to by his supporters to let go of their resentment toward him. I wanted us all to heal, for the good of the left and the future of our combined progress. Mr. Sanders nodded his head yes, rather begrudgingly, and we took the picture quickly, but not before he turned to an aide and said, "No more pictures. No more, I'm done, that's enough," ringing his hands for good measure. I couldn't help but imagine Hillary Clinton ever behaving like that (she wouldn't) and people just accepting it for what it is (they wouldn't).

Male politicians so rarely experience attacks based on their gender, but female politicians always do. Much is used against women that can never be used against men. It's important to give proper context to this pervasive inequality if we're really going to face it. At no time would it ever be possible to cause damage to a man's campaign or career by using some of the tactics used against a woman's campaign or career—such as implying Hillary Clinton was too physically weak to serve as president because she came down with pneumonia, or that what she wore or how she did her hair made her unlikable and therefore unrelatable, or that the actions, choices, or words of her partner were also things she must be held accountable for, or that accepting large fees for speaking engagements, the same type of fees famous men took all the time from companies on Wall Street, made her extremely untrustworthy and a shill. Even her voting record, which is the fairest reason to criticize her, is a voting record not unlike the likable Joe Biden's, nor did her policies differ from those adopted by Barack Obama during his presidency.

Shortly before the 2016 election, I was in Colorado campaigning for Hillary and making a round of phone calls to local voters at Clinton's campaign office alongside other surrogates and volunteers. I found myself on the phone begging one young female voter around my age to explain to me why she wouldn't vote for Hillary Clinton. "Look," the woman on the phone said, "you don't think I want to have a woman for president as much as you do? I do! I just don't want *that* woman. She is not who I imagined."

What do we imagine when we imagine a woman in a position of power, let alone the highest position in the country? Do we see her as she presents herself or do we see her as she has been projected? Which archetype must she fulfill in order to achieve such a position? Should she be an object of desire or an object of purity or both? Should she look less like our mothers or more like our daughters or wives, or none of these and just be a fantasy? Is she qualified only if her voting record is pristine, her past palatable, and her personality approachable? Must she be everything and nothing at the same time? A blank canvas and a revolutionary work of art, all in the same stroke?

In 2014, posters of Congresswoman Maxine Waters that deemed her a "Poverty Pimp" simply for buying herself a nice house were slathered all over Los Angeles. The posters were a double-edged sword of denigration in that they were racist and sexist at the same time. In 2013, Cécile Duflot, the French Minister of Territorial Equality and Housing, had to endure whistles from her male peers during a speech she was giving at the National Assembly because of a dress she was wearing. One of those men went so far as to blame Duflot for wearing something attractive as a ploy "so we wouldn't listen to what she was saying." Then there was the female conservative member of British Parliament who was told to be a good wife and not to disagree with her master (her husband) and a Sri Lankan UN Goodwill Ambassador who, after asking a question of a male parliament member, was told it was nice to answer a question from "a beauty queen." In 2018, freshman congresswoman Alexandria Ocasio-Cortez was shamed for wearing clothes deemed too nice for a woman from the Bronx who otherwise should be "struggling." It was the triple threat: racist, sexist, and classist.

Language to describe Hillary Clinton during both of her presidential campaigns ranged from ageist retorts to Wiccan conspiracies. Hillary had to face such enraging double standards as her qualifications were compared to those of *all* men who had ever run for president: She didn't have the commanding, lovable, curmudgeon's growl of Bernie Sanders or she didn't have the soft, reasonable voice of Obama's hope. Or she was no Bill Clinton. Or she was too much like Bill Clinton. Or she wasn't Fill-in-the-Blank-with-a-Male-Politician's-Name-Here.

This world demands nothing short of perfection from women who aim high, and our need to see perfection in women has, until recently, far outweighed our need for their participation. We need our successful women to be extremely successful but not self-made, and certainly not rich from being self-made. We need them to be only the best parts of the women we love and none of the worst parts of the women we hate. We need them to leave their husbands, to shut them up publicly, or to be better wives and stand by their husbands, to clean up their husband's mistakes and also face the consequences of their husbands' own mistakes.

The problem with having to rely on imagining what women can and cannot be is that we have to rely on exactly that: a form of make-believe. We have to envision it anew because it has never existed before. Since we've never actually experienced a woman in the highest office, it becomes routine to point at the very best we've got and say: "No thank you, you're still not good enough." Because we ourselves have been conditioned to hear the same of ourselves. No, thank you, you're still not good enough to get hired, or wear that dress, or direct that film, or be the CEO of this company, or give your opinion in general. We break down what represents us because we are used to being broken down. We keep women's flaws at the forefront of our decision-making, rather than women's intelligence and talent, thereby perpetuating the message that women have only imperfection to offer. And if we see this focus on our imperfections as an acceptable everyday norm, then we don't ever have to confront the spell—a spell that has cast women against one another, only seeing the other as flawed imperfections under the gaze that has been normalized for us. This makes us work against our own self-interests, forcing us to stay where we are. Leaving us to merely imagine what could be.

Although vastly different in many ways, the sharp parallels between my own difficult journey to success and Hillary Clinton's were impossible to ignore anymore. Every time I tried to verbalize these feelings to people who didn't agree, the pushback was doubly painful. My husband and I would get in such heated arguments about Hillary, deeply personal ones that at their core weren't even about the secretary, but about something far more alarming. We were really talking about two very different things. He was talking about Hillary Clinton the candidate, and I was talking about the Hillary Clinton that was me. When men criticized Hillary, it felt like all the ways in which we as women have ever been criticized. My defense of her, my understanding of her, my belief in her were all rooted in those same gut-level truths about myself. Because I had been her, in my career, in my life, in my own way. Almost everything she is and everything she went through could be applied or had been applied to me in one form or another. To feed into the hysteria, hyperbole, and melodrama of Hillary as some demonic archetype while asking women not to take personal offense or "become emotional" in our conversations was one of the most blatant forms of misogyny I have ever encountered. It was asking us not to feel for our own personal offenses.

And what is misogyny? Outside of its dictionary definition, what is it? How does it move in the world? Have you ever partaken in it, either knowingly or unknowingly? Are you sure? How can you be sure? If we as a society cannot even identify the many mercurial forms of misogyny and how it persists, then how can we possibly say what it isn't? How can we possibly tell women where and how it does not exist? How can we talk about the destruction of Hillary Clinton when we can't even talk about our own destruction? How are we expected to fully see her when we have lived full lives unseen?

When I hung up the phone with that young woman in Colorado, I felt a mixture of emotions but mostly a sense of despair. *How will this all end?* I wondered. By then Donald J. Trump had gnawed his way onto the Republican Party's center stage with the kind of personality and temperament that makes up most women's nightmares. He was every racist boss we ever worked for, every uncle we ever hid from, every man we would never, under any circumstances, marry. He personified not just the worst of mankind, but also the worst kind of man: the one in the store whose hand grazes your ass when walking by, or the one who crudely comments on your body and appearance during a meeting, or the one who tells you to smile, the one who talks over you, talks down to you, talks at you, talks through you. So I swallowed my anger. I swallowed my pain. I swallowed my disappointment. I picked up the phone and dialed the next number, shaken yet determined.

Requirements for a Woman
to Become President of the United States

I. Body language must read experienced yet
   teachable, strong but not forceful, embrace-
   able yet not mothering.

   A. No pulling strange faces or making eye-
      brow movements that imply insincerity
      or overt sincerity. Keep smiles between
      50 percent and 50.7 percent of their full
      width. Be careful of showing too many
      teeth, or too much tongue, or the inside of
      the mouth when laughing.

   B. Do not be stiff but do not exude too much
      freeness. Do not use any of the manner-
      isms men have used throughout politics,
      including but not limited to:

      i.   The thumbs-up while talking
      ii. Hand gestures when talking
      iii. Pointing
      iv. Waving

II. Voice must sound kind yet militant. Must not
    be grating to the ears. Must be commanding
    and strong but also warm and soothing.

    A. Voice must remain low in resonance
       and steady in vocal weight. (Baritone,
       for example.)

i. Voice octave level must stay between 47 and 55 decibels—never exceed this number or drop below it. <u>Don't whisper!</u>

ii. Under rare and unfortunate circumstances, such as during the female menstrual cycle, octave levels may exceed 55 decibels with a hard cap at 60 decibels, if she must.

iii. A shaky voice is illegal. Voice cracking is illegal. Vocal breaking is illegal. High pitch is illegal.

iv. Emotion is illegal.

v. Expressing sentiments such as "That is hurtful," or "I don't like the way you characterized me," or "I feel like you're not listening to me" is illegal. Any and all language expressing anger is illegal.

vi. Vulnerability is illegal.

vii. Punishments for tears include but are not limited to:

    a. Career damage

    b. Credibility destruction

    c. Public shaming

    d. Ousting from position or title

    e. Loss of trust

    f. Loss of merit

g. Loss of votes
h. Loss of endorsements
i. Being branded, which includes but is not limited to adjectives like:

1. Volatile, loose cannon, dramatic, crazy, hormonal, hysterical, unfit, disturbed, fickle, temperamental, frenzied, emotional, disorganized, raving mad, unpredictable, unreliable, unstable, hypersensitive, psychotic, high-strung, delicate, overreactive, moody, irritable, impulsive, testy, touchy, sore, turbulent, erratic, dicey, capricious, etc.

B. While speaking, be pointed but also off the cuff.
C. Speeches must have hope and reason and nuance and cadence yet also still feel dangerous and rogue.
D. Speech must sound worldly but also like that of a small-town girl. Eloquent and also tough. All-knowing but also open to the opinions of men.

III. Demeanor must be charismatic yet not subject to influence. Sex appeal is acceptable but

be non-feminine about it. Don't turn anyone
on! But don't turn anyone off!!

IV. Physical appearance must appease—and also
entice—everyone.

A. Shorter hair preferable but not too short,
hair-sprayed but not too ironed. More
bobs and fewer headbands or less mascu-
line and more cutting-edge. Hair should
exude corporateness and also be playful,
spunky but professional.

B. Clothing should be flattering but not
enticing. Attire should consist of strong
colors or neutral colors. No patterns and
no real sense of individuality. Stand out
from the crowd but don't break out of your
mold.

C. Wear necklines that show décolletage
but no cleavage, form-fitting attire that
is not masculine-presenting, bold looks,
vague pants, outfits that are subjectively
flattering and look great on you but only
according to other people. Do not wear
anything unattractive, or hideous, or un-
appealing, or too tight, or too smart, or too
expensive, or generic, or dreadful, or an
eyesore, or indicative of aunties or great-
grandmothers. Wear something slightly
sexy that makes you desirable or sassy. For

definitions and qualifications of these examples, see: Men.

D. Do not have wrinkles on the face, neck, elbows, wrists, hands, fingers, sternum, chest, back, thighs, calves, ankles, feet, toes, or vagina.

E. Never mention your vagina! You do not have one! You are not defined by one!

F. Vaginas are illegal!

V. Make sure that your voting record is absolutely pristine, with absolutely no mistakes, bad judgment calls, or excuses. If you have held public office (see item VI, below) previously, your voting record should be centrist-liberal yet Socialist Democrat at the same time, or it should be centrist-conservative while also being Libertarian. Your voting record needs to be psychic and all-seeing. The votes must reflect everything that will ever happen in the future and must be mindful of everything that's ever happened in the past.

VI. You must have prior history and experience in public office in order to be considered qualified. To be qualified to run as a woman you must have the following:

A. Military service, tenure as a teacher, tenure as a federal judge, tenure as a mayor, tenure as a governor, tenure as a mother, a law degree, a bachelor's degree, an associate's degree, a master's degree, a doctorate, an MBA, a Pulitzer Prize, and an EGOT.

B. You must be pro-everything and also anti-everything at the same time: pro-choice, pro-taxes, pro—military spending, pro-ACLU and pro-NRA, pro—Medicare for all, pro—budget cuts, pro—capital punishment, pro-life, pro-union, pro—renewable energy, pro-organic, pro-gluten-free, pro-immigration, pro-corporations, pro-government, pro—human rights, pro—gay marriage, pro-men.

C. Be white.

8

Do you remember where you were when you heard the audio clip? "And when you're a star, you can do it. You can do anything—grab them by the pussy, do anything."

I was sitting on the bed in a hotel room in Montclair, California, where my film *Paint It Black* had just played at a festival, when Trump's audio recording came blaring through the TV. I watched in horror as the entire audiotape was played. A sickening feeling came over me and I grabbed my stomach, almost hoping to shield my unborn daughter from his words. A guy who used to be a very close friend and who I knew was a Trump supporter texted me about a film he had just seen, and I used the opportunity to ask him what he thought of the tape. Since he had a young daughter, did it change his mind about his candidate in any way? He wrote me back and told me to leave his daughter out of politics and that what Trump had said were "just words." This was a man I had known and been neighbors with for almost a decade, whose family I had spent time with and whose wife I was close with. It was the last time I ever spoke to him. Had he been this way the whole time and I just ignored it? Had most men I knew been like this the whole time and I just ignored it?

That night, just before boarding a flight back to New York, I was so upset that I shared a story on my Instagram account that would change my life forever. It was a story about an event from when I was twenty-one years old, involving an ex-boyfriend with whom I had had a very tumultuous, abusive relationship. I recounted a time when, after breaking up, he found me in a club and picked me up around the neck with one hand and used the other to grab me by the vagina and drag me toward the exit. "This is mine," he shouted in my ear as he pulled me outside. The girlfriends I had come with ran after him, pounding on his back to let me go. Between them and his two brothers, who were also there that night, they were able to pry him off of me. A security guard walked us to my car and it was then that I looked down and realized my grandmother's necklace, which I always wore, had been ripped off in the struggle. I didn't dare go back inside to find it. I was completely numb, in shock. I looked down at my dress and saw that it was covered in blood. Was it my blood? Then I remembered his face, his mouth covered in blood after fighting with security, who'd held him back as he screamed at me that this was my fault. That I had done this to him.

The next morning, my vagina was so sore, I googled how to make a sitz bath, something traditionally used by women after giving vaginal birth. I sat in the shallow bathwater and stared at the faucet. I didn't cry. I was numb.

After I posted this story on Instagram, I landed in New York six hours later to large news coverage of my post and dozens of articles written about my sexual assault. I stared at those words—*sexual assault*—and realized I had never called it that before, not even in my own head. I had always told myself the experience was just a physical assault. The thought of it being sexual never even occurred to me. That's when it dawned on me: I had unconsciously mischaracterized my own abuse as something less intimate and therefore tolerable. If it was a *physical* assault, I likely didn't ask for it. But if it was a *sexual* assault, there's a good chance I did. And had I understood it to be that kind of assault back then, when it happened—the kind I may have *earned*—then that means I could've been complicit in all the other acts of violence I endured in that relationship as well.

When I got home I finally cried. David held me.

I was later forced to talk to my own father about it, after receiving a text from my mom that said, "Hey, honey. Dad just saw your story on the evening news and he's very upset. Please call us when you can." My Instagram post was flooded with thousands upon thousands of comments by women and some men all over the world sharing similar stories of harassment and abuse. It felt powerful, necessary, and dangerous—the voices of so many moving in on the silence of their abuse like a catastrophic wave.

Shortly after the story went viral, the ex-boyfriend in question found me on an old private Facebook account through mutual friends. He messaged me to apologize for what had happened between us all those years before and went on to tell me I had perhaps exaggerated the experiences of violence in our relationship. It took me several days to decide whether responding to him would be worth it, and in the end, I did, but not without consequence—the consequence of me turning on myself and my decision to speak out. Even in writing him back and correcting him, telling him that I definitely did not exaggerate what happened to me, I left the conversation feeling like I had done the wrong thing by saying anything publicly in the first place. I had gone to great lengths to protect his identity and not out him by name in the story of what had happened to me, but I still felt guilty for dredging up his horrible behavior from the past when we had both moved on and he had a young child of his own now. I was angry and felt estranged from myself. I questioned whether this incident really did happen the way I had framed it, all while knowing full well it undeniably did.

What is it about sexual violence that leaves survivors feeling like they somehow deserved their abuse? And what is it about our culture that perpetuates this blame and sends the message that it's okay to shame survivors into believing they are somehow responsible for what's been done to them? For women, these have been historically difficult questions with answers that lie in the foundational belief that the autonomy of our bodies is not ours to govern in the first place. That even the judgment of our physical selves belongs to the patriarchal point of view and is reserved for those in positions of power—predominantly men—who decide everything from how we are supposed to look, to whether our experiences are real or not, to how we are allowed to feel. We have been treated like objects to be acquired and disposed of based on those desires, and I imagine that those in the queer community—most especially in the trans community—have had to shoulder a very similar kind of burden, except they've also had to fight for the basic recognition of their gender.

Last year, the nomination of Judge Brett Kavanaugh to the Supreme Court came to a screeching halt when a woman, Dr. Christine Blasey Ford, came forward, accusing him of sexually assaulting her when they were teenagers. The reaction from members of the Senate Judiciary Committee, and even the president of the United States, aimed to discredit her before she had stepped into the room to testify. President Trump tweeted asserting that she must have documented this egregious act at some point—she must have proof. Surely she didn't just let a seventeen-year-old Kavanaugh cover her mouth and pin her down while his friend watched without reporting it to the authorities, right?

Donald Trump himself has been accused by nearly two dozen women of sexual assault and harassment, and the most telling indication of our country's collective consciousness is that many Americans didn't even bat an eye when they found out. We do not see the sexual assault epidemic as a worthwhile fight because we see the bodies of minorities, women, and the LGBTQIA community as unworthy causes; the nation's apathy toward survivors of sexual assault stems directly from our indifference toward the people it predominantly effects.

By the end of the 2016 campaign, after Donald Trump's remarks about grabbing pussies and doing whatever he wanted because he's a star, I had turned into one flaring nerve among millions of others, seizing together in the united body of womankind.

Trump's words had blown us all wide open, igniting our long-silenced traumas into a newfound, boiling rage. What was coming had been coming for generations and was long overdue. It was the beginning of a revolution. A revolution that finally belonged to its revolutionaries: women of all kinds.

9

It was the night of the 2016 election and the energy inside the Javits Center in New York City was charged with excitement, anxiety, and wild, ferocious joy. I was standing in a room full of fellow Hillary Clinton surrogates and supporters, surrounded by men and women who had literally spent years working on her 2016 bid for the presidency, which we now believed we were about to win. I stood in a small circle smiling and laughing with America Ferrera and our friend Amy Schumer. We all happened to show up to the occasion wearing matching white pantsuits complete with white blazers, looking like the cast of some new primetime medical drama. "On an all-new *San Bernardino Medical,* Friday nights on NBC!" America was drinking Champagne, Amy was double-fisting two plastic cups of Chardonnay, and I was enjoying a lovely cup of liquid Zantac. (I was seven-and-a-half-months pregnant and on my third consecutive month of severe heartburn.) Mary Steenburgen arrived with her husband, Ted Danson, and we immediately locked eyes from across the room. Tonight was the night. We were going to make history.

It wasn't long before the mood in the room began to change as news started to trickle in that Hillary was losing. I swigged some more Zantac. My baby shoved her foot into my ribs as if to foreshadow that more pain was on its way. The Clinton staff huddled in corners, whispering. Katy Perry anxiously chewed on a celery stick. Kate McKinnon, who earlier had been the life of the party, now stood quietly by herself looking over the balcony. Below her were a sea of thousands of heartbroken faces: husbands and wives with kids wearing I'M WITH HER T-shirts, farmers who had driven in from neighboring states, drag queens in blond Hillary wigs and pantsuits, a Nick Nolte impersonator or, perhaps, Nick Nolte himself.

We watched until well after midnight as each state's results came in and the outlook became more and more grim. Finally, Adrienne Elrod, Hillary Clinton's director of strategic communications for the campaign, came over to let us know that Hillary would not be coming to the Javits Center and that we should all start heading home. "We don't know yet what the outcome is, but we won't know until the morning," she told us. But we knew. We all knew.

Our shocked realization that she had lost the presidency was rocked by an even more awful realization: If Hillary had lost, that meant Donald Trump had won. Donald Trump—a sexual assaulter, a con man, a billionaire with ties to Russian oligarchs, who rated women's looks on a numbered scale, who called Mexicans "rapists," who told black people to vote for him because they had nothing else to lose, whose most worthwhile contribution to society was hosting a reality show—was going to be our next president.

I looked at America from across the room. We stared at each other, breathing heavily, sickened, astonished. We held each other's gaze as if to say: What now? What the hell are we going to do now?

After Hillary's defeat, Mary and Ted offered to drive me and my friend Mindy back home. We were silent in the car. Stunned. Numb. Mary finally broke the silence by saying, "I don't think I've felt this much pain since my mother died."

The next morning I got on the subway to head to a meeting in Midtown Manhattan and the world felt like a tableau of itself, a frozen painting of sorrow. It had shattered overnight and every face around me was a slivered shard. I looked at the people across from me on the A train and they numbly stared back, eyes red and swollen like mine. My heart began to pound as a dark realization swarmed over me. I was going to bring a baby into the world. And not just any baby, a girl. And not just any world, *this* world of racism. The world of deeply ingrained misogyny. The world of Donald Trump's order.

My heart sunk as I quietly said to myself that maybe I didn't want this baby after all. I thought, *I can give her away to Canadians. Or to a nice family in Sweden. The Swedes make really good furniture; they must raise really good children, too.* I told myself I couldn't bear the thought of bringing a girl into this new, terrifying world, that I loved her more than I could bear and wanted to protect her from all of this.

I started to feel light-headed. Twenty minutes later I stepped out of the train—waddled, rather—and felt my legs quiver beneath me. My stomach lurched and I began to sweat. Something wasn't right. I began to climb the stairs at the Columbus Circle exit and a deep, piercing pain slithered through my spine. I grabbed the railing and groaned. *My God,* I thought, *this is it. I'm going into labor. I'm going into fucking labor in a subway stairwell.* I couldn't catch my breath and sat down on a step halfway up the staircase. I was breathing hard, clutching my stomach, and crying.

A homeless man emerged from around the corner, carrying a duffel bag and a plastic bag full of fruit. "Oh, shit. It's going DOWN!" he hollered when he saw me. A few more people stopped and came to my side, asking concerned questions, none of which I could hear or comprehend in my dazed state. All I could do was gasp and wheeze and cry. "Listen," the homeless man said to some bystanders, "I can help cut an umbilical cord if anyone needs me to. I have beard scissors! I just need some Purell if anybody has any." *My God,* I thought, *this is it. I'm going into labor in a fucking stairwell and a homeless man is going to cut my cord with his beard clippers.*

Another man identified himself as an off-duty paramedic and asked if I thought I might be going into labor. "I don't . . . I don't know," I said between attempts to catch my breath. "Either . . . either Hillary Clinton broke my water or Donald Trump just gave me a miscarriage."

I was scared and hyperventilating. Two men helped me to the top of the stairwell, where I could get cell service and call my doctor. I sat on the curb and dialed her number. The homeless man followed and pulled an orange out of his plastic bag and placed it on the edge of the curb near me in a gesture of kindness. He nodded and walked away.

I did not go into labor that day. In fact, I was not having contractions at all—I was having a massive panic attack. My doctor, Lee, instructed me to come directly to her office, which I did. "Okay, kiddo," she said in her tough Jersey accent. "Give it to me. What's going on?"

I told my doctor that Hillary Clinton's loss for me

was not just about the loss of a candidate I admired, it was a critical loss for America's identity. It was a robbery of womankind. Her loss was a projection of all of our losses, as women, throughout history; a culmination of our collective sacrifices, our abuses, our disparities, our silences, and our injustices. Hillary was the cherry on top, symbolic of all that we had fought for, for generations. I told her I didn't know how to raise a daughter in that kind of loss. That kind of void.

When you are about to become a mother, people tell you to expect many things. Expect to be exhausted all the time, to lose a lot of sleep, to never have sex with your husband, all of which is true—especially if your husband was a Bernie supporter—but no one ever tells women how incredibly vulnerable they will feel. That you live in a perpetual state of rawness, of constant fear for your child and the life that child will live or miss out on or never get to live at all. No one prepares you for the type of love you will experience, because it cannot be explained.

I didn't know how to love something—*someone*—that much, so much that it owned me. I told my doctor I was so confused. I felt estranged from myself and the world I had once lived in. I asked her if I could take anything—any antianxiety medication or even one sip of bourbon—in order to quell the sadness. In order not to feel so much, all the time.

". . . Okay, kiddo, you done?" she said to me

sharply. "Listen, we're gonna do something right now, okay? We're gonna do something for you and that worn-out head of yours."

She placed a heart monitor on my stomach and told me to pull out my iPhone. She proceeded to tell me I could do whatever I wanted all day long—I could torture myself by reading the news, watching the inauguration, reading Twitter: "Go nuts," she said. "But I want you to do two things every day. Every morning when you first wake up and every night right before you go to bed, I want you to play the recording of your daughter's heart beating for yourself and remember your own capacity to love. How deeply, dangerously, and daringly we all choose to love in this merciless world, no matter its cruelties."

I began to cry.

"I love her so much, Lee," I said. "How can I keep her safe?"

"You can't," she said. "But you can keep her close."

She pressed record on my phone's voice memo app and we recorded the sound of my daughter's small heartbeat for two full minutes. Its tiny thump pounding along like a small train gearing up for life's most treacherous track. Her blood swirling around in a muffled slush, wholly new, preparing her body to enter into a world still broken, still in need of so much piecing together, but unlike anything the women who came before her had ever known.

10

"You can't go," my doctor Lee said firmly over the phone, "you're two weeks away from your due date and I can't let you travel."

"Even to fight the patriarchy?"

"Even to fight the patriarchy."

What my doctor didn't know, and still doesn't know (until now maybe . . . sorry, Lee), is that I was making this phone call while already traveling. It was January 2017, and I had called her from the train bound for DC to attend the first Women's March. My daughter was hiccuping inside me, and I placed a hand on where I imaged her mouth was and felt for the tiny oscillations of her lungs. I knew I was making the right move, however risky. I knew if I went into labor during the march, I'd certainly be in the

right company, surrounded by a pink sea of gyne-
cologists and midwives. Arguably it was the best
place to be if my water *did* break. All I'd have to do
is shoot some kind of vaginal bat-signal up into the
sky—a feminist flare gun—and I'd be surrounded by
a plethora of doulas within seconds.

I arrived in DC on Inauguration Day, the day
before the march, and the energy in the city was
charged with hostility. It didn't feel like a day of celebration. It felt like a day of retaliation. Police outfit-
ted in riot gear were lining the streets, and extremist
groups protested by smashing windows and lighting
cars on fire. There were the Brown Berets, ANTIFAS,
and black bloc groups, anarchists and nihilists alike,
all swarming among Trump supporters and enthu-
siasts in an unsettling hive of aggression. And then
there was me, almost nine months pregnant, with
my friend Katie Jacobs, pushing through a human
chain of activists at the entrance of the inauguration site just so I could get to the Dunkin' Donuts on
the other side. I pulled two people's hands apart and
shoved my bulging stomach through as they chanted
"No justice, no peace." There would be no justice and
definitely no peace if I didn't eat something soon.

That night I huddled in a hotel room with Katie
and some of my closest friends, musician Emily
Wells and her partner, the artist Samantha Nye, as
well as Latina poet Rachel McKibbens and three of
her children. Katie got us a large suite and we asked

management to bring in extra cots so we could all shack up together. We sat around drawing our protest signs and preparing for the next day, all while watching what was happening outside on the street play out on the news. We didn't know what the next day would bring in light of the intensity in the air, but the anxiety didn't deter us. We felt safer in numbers. We knew that what we were there to fight for was not a fight that we could wage alone, and that the more voices joining the outcry, the louder the message to be heard would be.

Attending protests of this magnitude is not some weekend getaway or a bandwagon to get on or a fad to exploit. They are large-scale dialogues on survival—a way to directly and loudly impact a world that often has a hard time listening. People gather in public spaces to march in protest not just because they are angry and want things to change, but because they don't want to be alone in that fight and that feeling. There is comfort in the knowledge that solidarity exists, but there is relief and deep gratification in actually seeing it manifest, face-to-face, body-by-body.

When I stepped onto the train bound for DC that weekend, the first thing I saw was a car completely full of women en route to the march. All *kinds* of women. There were women in full pink pussy garb and then there were women in suits just getting off work, pulling RESIST pins out of their briefcases and pinning them to their lapels. There was a group of rowdy aunties in matching sweaters, and a lone millennial working on her computer that bore a sticker saying A WOMAN'S PLACE IS IN THE RESISTANCE. I sat down in my row and noticed that the woman in front of me was sitting next to her preteen daughter and talking on the phone with her husband. "No, we don't know where we're staying yet, but I'm sure we can crash with Maria," she said. "All of our friends are here, you know that. The whole world is here right now, even if just in spirit."

"Let me talk to him," her daughter interrupted.

"Hang on, Octavia wants to say hi."

The little girl got on the phone and her father asked her a question. She answered, "Because this is very important."

"This is important."

Hillary's words from that Post-it note echoed; she and this little girl were right. This *was* important—showing up, together, and fighting for our livelihood—this was how we began to draw that early line in the sand. How we began to show the world, under this new president and any power structure like him, exactly what side of that line we stood on and exactly what kind of weapons we were going to wield against their war on women.

Women's bodies have always been the prisoners of wars we did not wage: wars of ownership, choice, sexual violence, fantasy, and definition. We have been prisoners of the war on physical appearance, which has dictated how we look and dress and how much we weigh, and we have been prisoners of the war on creative expression, which decides our artistic merit and value. These battles against us are wars of attrition, fought for centuries, aiming to grind us down into rubble piles of our own principles.

In order for us to break free from this prison system of the body and mind, we must return to the root of who we are, away from the architects of our cells. We have always been nurturers, though we have not been permitted to really explore what, exactly, nurturing means *to us,* not just to our families and communities. As women, yes, we nurture our children and our partners and the people we love. But we must also nurture our right to reject those archetypes and the notion of nurturing altogether. We should nurture that right. We must take care of our careers, our power, and our ambition, as well as our right to be imperfect, difficult, and sometimes even bad people.

THE MORNING AFTER Donald Trump's inauguration, the sky pierced blue and a calmness befell DC. As my friend Katie and I drove to a pre-march morning event hosted by then-president of Planned Parenthood Cecile Richards, a brightness began to leak into the city as people covered from head to toe in shades of pink poured out into the streets. As we got closer to the event, the crowds began to double then triple in size. The street we were driving along eventually became so filled with people that the taxi had to pull over, and Katie and I walked the remaining several blocks to meet up with screenwriter Callie Khouri of *Thelma & Louise* and *Nashville* fame.

After the breakfast finished, I stepped out onto the sidewalk to find rivers of people dressed in lilacs, reds, and magentas walking down every road as far as the eye could see. Cars, houses, and trees appeared to be floating among them as though consumed by a flood of bright color. I had never seen anything like it.

Cecile asked if we wanted a ride to the march and we gratefully accepted. On the way, Cecile, Katie, Callie, and I discussed how angry this moment in history had made us as mothers (or in my case, a mother-to-be), as though we were going backward in time, as though with the cast of a ballot so much of what each of us and the women before us had fought for was instantly being erased. "Look at all of them," Cecile said as she stared out the window at the people filling the streets, headed to the march. Her face stirred with joy, a smile breaking across it. "Okay. I'm feeling better now. Seeing them is making me feel better." We turned a corner, and a group of women and men holding up WOMEN'S RIGHTS ARE HUMAN RIGHTS signs spotted Cecile in her fluorescent pink suit and immediately began to scream with elation. "We love you, Cecile!" one woman yelled. "We're here for you and what you've done for us!" Our van came to a stop right in front of them at the entrance of the march, and Cecile stepped out of the van as all of us followed behind her. She walked right up to the woman, looked her in the eyes, and said, "And I am here for you. Always."

The intention put forth that day was happening not just in DC, but all over the world. My mother marched with her friends in downtown Los Angeles while my sixteen-year-old niece made signs with her friends and marched in San Francisco. I had friends marching across the world, in England, Ireland, and France. And as each of us was joined by more like minds, moving in crowds alongside hundreds of thousands of strangers with one common goal. The more connected we felt, the stronger we became.

For many, Donald Trump's election was the grenade that exploded us into a second civil rights movement, but for me and many other women like me, Hillary Clinton's loss was the pulling of that grenade's pin. Both Hillary the candidate and Hillary the woman. Her loss ignited an ancient female fury, fueled by generations of egregious inequality, smothered identity, and ritual abuse. People marched not just because of what Donald Trump did, but because of what all the Donald Trumps have always done. Women marched not just because a woman had lost, but because we too were all done with losing.

No matter how anyone feels about Mrs. Clinton

as a candidate, we can all agree—*must* agree—that atrocious and flagrant sexism played a massive part in the 2016 election. It plays a part in every attempt by women to gain access or authority in any industry and under any title. Love her or hate her, Mrs. Clinton's misogynistic defeat sent a message to women everywhere: If *she* can't succeed—this highly qualified yet imperfect woman—then *none* of us can succeed. And if we cannot succeed, we cannot survive.

The first Women's March was not just Donald Trump's forewarning, it was America's foreshadowing of what was to come: a new era for the nation—and for me.

11

was sitting at a hotel desk in London, writing on my computer, in the early fall of 2016 when I felt a small ache throbbing in the crevice between my thumb and my wrist. I shook it off, massaged my hand, ran it under hot water—as hot as I could stand—and the ache went away. But the next day, it returned. Soon it spread to my other fingers and even up my forearm, making my whole hand tingle with numbness. At night, a sharp pain in my wrist would keep me up for hours, and during the day, my hand would flush red one minute, then moments later, white and cold as a corpse. I lived with the strange pain for several more weeks and continued to write, wearing a brace I bought from a local pharmacy.

Upon returning to the States, I was diagnosed

with a pretty severe case of something called De Quervain's syndrome, otherwise known as Black-Berry Thumb, an inflammation of the tendons in the thumb and wrist. My doctor told me this was common in pregnant women due to a hormone called relaxin that's released in the latter half of pregnancy. Relaxin forces the joints and ligaments in a woman's body to start . . . relaxing, which allows for the pelvis to move and the cervix to begin softening and widening so as to make way for the baby's body during birth. But relaxin can also cause adverse side effects for people who use repetitive motions, such as, say, writing a novel.

As my stomach grew, so did the pain. My osteopathic doctor, Mary Banyo, prescribed "bed rest" for my hand—little to no typing and some stretching exercises—but general, everyday use had caused the pain to spread into my other hand as well. I auditioned several brands of wrist and thumb braces and became an expert in the world of splints. I tried copper compression gloves, which purport to help regrow the joint cartilage by absorbing copper metal into the skin. I tried kinesiology tape, a roll of strong adhesive that you put directly on the skin to hold muscle and bone in place. None of it worked so I went back to the basic splint gloves. The best one I found was from a CVS Pharmacy brand called Futuro, which had discreet thumb splints that didn't bend, and I could hide them under long-sleeved sweaters in public. I wore them on both hands all night and for most of the day for the next two months. I became very fond of my Futuro splints and didn't mind having a codependent relationship with them. I even gave them a pet name, my Futchies, and would freely refer to them as such, my initial embarrassment giving way to some kind of demented pride. We needed each other. I needed them to protect my hands and they needed me to press "Delicates" on the washer when cleaning them.

But as much as I loved my Futchies, they made it nearly impossible to carry out daily tasks, so my cousin-in-law Aviva came to live with me for a month while David was still away in London. Aviva was extremely helpful around the house, from helping me get dressed to doing the grocery shopping. I don't know what I would have done without her. But I had to cease writing my novel for the time being, and that was devastating. Aviva had to send emails for me, order items for the baby's room, and walk my dog three times a day, as my dog Ollie would often pull on the leash, sending a flushed pain up my arm. I felt so helpless, so useless, and so frustrated. Most simple tasks would usually devolve into me kicking over something I couldn't physically grasp in frustration and bursting into tears. My doctors told me that I just had to wait it out, that after the birth, all of my symptoms would disappear with the natural alleviation of inflammation in my body.

There are many ways in which women are disenfranchised and erased in our day-to-day lives, but one of the biggest and perhaps least discussed is the deprivation of basic education and information about the tolls taken on our bodies when birthing children, tolls that are often fatal. For women of color in America, this is especially true. Black women are three times more likely to die during childbirth than white women, and until the Affordable Care Act was passed in 2010, black women experienced much higher rates of heart disease mortality, AIDS, diabetes, and many other preventable diseases.

A 2017 study by the Institute for Women's Policy Research found that white women have the highest incidence rates of cancer in the country, but black women still have the highest death rates from cancer. Much of this is due to the fact that black women are much less likely to receive preventive care. Minority women have been all but excluded from clinical studies, especially those pertaining to heart disease and cancer. Women in America have been illegally tested on, denied access to reproductive health care, and just plain ignored for generations.

There have always been huge gender inequalities in research and education in the medical world. My friend Meredith, an emergency medicine physician, put it very simply to me recently: "Textbook medicine has always been taught with a white male focus." Most diseases are broken up into a gendered hierarchy that sounds more like the title of a John Gray relationship advice book than actual science: *Men Are from "Symptoms We Have Answers For," Women Are from "We Wish We Could Help You."* A 1998 study titled "Integrating the Gender Perspective in Medical and Health Education and Research," published for the United Nations, found that diseases that afflict mostly men have fairly straightforward and well-researched symptoms and, therefore, diagnoses, whereas diseases that afflict women are far less understood, with symptoms often misdiagnosed, misconstrued, or altogether ignored. Women are more likely to be affected by more precarious diseases, such as nerve disorders or perplexing autoimmune diseases. For instance, women are three times more likely to be diagnosed with rheumatoid arthritis than men, and they exclusively suffer from fibromyalgia and other chronic autoimmune diseases that have little research behind what instigates them, let alone how to treat them.

There are very real reasons why women are more susceptible to certain diseases than men are, one of which is the X chromosome and its many genes related to the immune system. While this is an unavoidable reality, I take issue with the lack of research and the real gender bias when it comes to the treatment of women and their bodies. Men pretty much know everything there is to know about their genitalia from a young age, and anything they are not taught by a parent or school, they are taught through society and entertainment. Conversely, the entirety of the female clitoris was discovered only recently, in 2009. (Before then, it was believed to be solely the small button of flesh inside the labia, but in fact, a French scientist found that the clitoris is more than ten centimeters long and extends deep inside the vaginal canal.) Men have free access to Viagra and other forms of erectile dysfunction drugs through our health care system, but women have to fight like hell just to get birth control covered. Men have no laws governing their physical bodies. Women have more than we can count.

Why does modern medicine, led by male doctors, see the study and treatment of women's bodies as less important?

The physician Bernadine Healey wrote a powerful editorial in *The New England Journal of Medicine* in 1991, which she began by saying, "Yentl, the nineteenth-century heroine of Isaac Bashevis Singer's short story, had to disguise herself as a man to attend school and study the Talmud. Being 'just like a man' has historically been a price women have had to pay for equality. Being different from men has meant being second class and less than equal for most of recorded time and throughout most of the world. It may therefore be sad, but not surprising, that women have all too often been treated less than equally in social relations, political endeavors, business, education, research, and health care." Healey goes on to examine two studies, also printed in *The New England Journal of Medicine,* that show how deeply biased the medical industry is in favor of the health and well-being of men over women. And since that editorial was published more than three decades ago, much remains the same, from male-dominated medical teams, staff, and boards of directors of hospitals, to the medical research they all rely on, which has historically and overwhelmingly favored the male body over the female body.

A team of three professors from Harvard, the University of Michigan, and Washington University recently published a fascinating study in the Proceedings of the National Academy of Sciences of the United States (PNAS) showing that women are statistically more likely to survive heart attacks if they are treated by female doctors, and male doctors are more effective when they have more female colleagues in the room. The study looked at 500,000 heart attack patients admitted to hospital emergency departments in Florida between 1991 and 2010, and it found that female patients treated by male physicians were less likely to survive than patients of either gender treated by female physicians or male patients treated by male physicians. The study also found that survival rates among female patients treated by male physicians had far better outcomes when there were more female physicians present in the emergency department working alongside the male physicians. The study also looked at previous findings, which showed that female physicians often performed better overall than male physicians across a wide variety of ailments that affect both men and women. "If female patients tend to be more challenging for male and female doctors to diagnose and treat," the professors wrote in the PNAS study, "the patterns we document may reflect the fact that the most skillful physicians (i.e., female physicians) provide the highest return to their skills when treating the most challenging patients (i.e., female patients)."

So why aren't there more women physicians, more women running hospitals, more women in the boardrooms and emergency rooms? Enter the mantra: Long-term chronic sexism. The same kind of sexism that allows male leaders in the medical field to disregard diseases that predominantly afflict women. One of the most blatant ways in which the world tells women: we are "less than" might be simply by working to make sure the health of men, and the men in power who enforce men's health care and medical research, are "more than."

If we want equality and inclusivity in medicine,

and if we want to see better results both for women in the field of medicine and for women who are patients, we need to see more female representation in leadership positions and in what research is being funded. Lack of representation is always—ALWAYS—the problem, in any field, in any industry. Data from the Association of American Medical Colleges shows that while 46 percent of applicants to medical school are women, the percentage dramatically decreases for academic positions held by women, with only 38 percent of actual faculty members, 21 percent of full professors, and 16 percent of deans being women. Female physicians are also paid less than their male peers, who have better RVU (relative value unit) rates, often for doing the exact same work as male physicians.

Women are also more likely to be afflicted by mental health problems than men, though men are far more likely to have drug and alcohol problems. Issues like depression affect one in four women, while affecting only one in ten men. Women are also twice as likely as men to experience anxiety disorders.

In all, women do not have the same access to information about their health care choices, often because the information simply does not exist. We need to invest not only in women's futures and voices, but in women's bodies, too. Mothers especially should be afforded more knowledge about the physical toll childbirth takes postpartum.

MY DAUGHTER, Marlow Alice Cross, was delivered by scheduled C-section in February 2017, on Susan B. Anthony's birthday. Before going into the operating room, I took off my Futchies for the last time so an IV could be administered into the top of my hand. "Goodbye my little F-words," I told them. "Thank you for taking care of my paws for so long." I threw them in the waste bin and prepared to be gifted twofold, with a brand-new baby girl and my old hands back.

After giving birth, many symptoms left my body. My acid reflux vanished and so did the sciatica in my leg. The pain in my wrists was also gone. Or so I thought. I was on heavy pain and anti-inflammatory medications for the first few days after surgery, and by the time they started to wear off, the pain started to creep back. Within two weeks, I had full-blown bilateral De Quervain's syndrome and carpal tunnel in both hands. My doctors were flummoxed. I was sent to see Moussia Krinsky-Raskin, a physical therapist specializing in hand rehabilitation. She made me a pair of hard plastic gloves that conformed to the exact shape of my hands and that had big Velcro buckles to hold them in place—Futchies Supreme. There was nothing discreet about them. They were thick and bulky and would draw an entire subway car's attention when I'd adjust the massive Velcro straps with their loud tearing noise. I looked and sounded like some off-brand Marvel superheroine, only not *super* at all, and hardly a *heroine.*

Before I had Marlow, life with my Futchies was frustrating but doable. But Futchies Supreme presented huge obstacles and made new motherhood extremely difficult. In the early stages of breastfeeding, even with Marlow latched onto my nipple, I'd have to rhythmically compress my breast to get the milk flowing (this is called expressing), which was impossible to do while wearing the hard plastic gloves.

It wasn't just the feedings that were difficult. Holding my newborn naturally also proved nearly impossible. I'd have to use the undersides of my forearms to pick up her small body, clasping her between them like two slices of bread for a sandwich. Sometimes I would hit her in the head with the hard edges of the gloves when trying to stroke her hair or adjust my breast in her mouth. She'd cry. Again I'd have to grasp her between my forearms and carefully maneuver picking her up, hands free, to comfort her. Putting her clothes on was also a challenge, and the simple act of snapping the clasps on her onesie became a ten-minute, sweat-inducing task ending in frustration and tears. I'd use my middle and index fingers like some sad crab, slowly pushing the buttons together while she squirmed and kicked. And when I put diapers on her, they looked like some mangled towel caught in a tire compared to my husband's perfect diapering capabilities. If no one was home and I had no help, I'd just have to take the gloves off entirely and deal with the burning and throbbing in my arms.

Months of physical therapy went by with little to no change. I'd work with Moussia twice a week doing exercises and stretches, ending each session by icing my arms and using pulsed electromagnetic field therapy to redirect the pain. I'd have sessions with Dr. Mary Bayno, who spent much of her treatment working on the muscles in my arms, wrists, and hands. I worked with a wonderful acupuncturist and healer named Vickie Lee, who had helped tremendously during my pregnancy and was now working vigorously to get the inflammation out of my body. Three times a day I would soak my hands in hot water, Epsom salt, and magnesium for twenty minutes using my daughter's Tupperware bottle-washing bowl, which was lightweight and the perfect size for my hands.

For eight months after giving birth, my hands felt like they were never going to return to normal. I was tested for every autoimmune disease possible, from rheumatoid arthritis to Hashimoto's disease,

Lyme disease to thyroid conditions, but every test came back negative. I consulted with an orthopedic surgeon, who gave me cortisone shots in my wrists, which proved pointless. I had my hands X-rayed to check for arthritis and got electromyography (EMG) to see if some unknown nerve damage was perhaps the cause. I used CBD oils and arnica creams and turmeric and the Chinese therapy *gua sha* (scraping) and cupping and Rolfing and everything you could possibly think of to try to get my body to heal.

Then one day, at the suggestion of several healers I had been working with, I took off the plastic gloves and left them off. I left them off and worked through the weeks upon weeks of tingling and numbness and pain. Slowly, the symptoms started to ease, and one day, the pain in my hands, wrists, and arms was gone. Just like that. It left my body as swiftly as it came.

Vickie had maintained from the first day we worked together that I had no autoimmune diseases or any other kind of damage, but rather fairly normal, postpartum inflammation that was taking longer than usual to leave my body. "Women aren't taught enough about their bodies," she said during one of our first sessions. "You are *full* of inflammation right now, as you should be. You just had a child."

"Well, I didn't *just* have a child. I had her almost a year ago," I said.

"Yes, but we women need real time to heal,

sometimes a year or more. This world hates our bodies so much, they want us to bounce back a few days after we give birth and act like nothing ever happened. They think we want to have it all—including the suffering! Do not feel guilty. Be kind to yourself . . . this world will not be."

For many women who choose to become mothers, guilt—along with our newborn children—suddenly becomes the center of our world, virtually overnight. Most mothers I know have felt like they aren't doing it right, or aren't good enough at it, or aren't strong enough, or aren't providing enough, or are selfish if they take time away from their babies, or are failures if they don't raise or feed their babies the way other mothers do.

Why does this happen to us? Certainly fathers feel guilt too, that is without question; but mothers take it to such an extreme it sometimes completely overshadows the joy that they should feel instead. I myself dealt with extreme feelings of inadequacy and guilt in ways I had never even come close to before. The sudden overwhelming vulnerability I felt when I became a mother was breathtaking and took the shell of armor I had spent two decades building for myself and threw it out the window. Nothing could've possibly prepared me for how exposed I felt the minute Marlow left my body and entered the world.

Since breastfeeding was difficult for me, I often had to pump instead. And because Marlow was not breastfeeding as much as I would have liked, soon my milk began to dry up and then was gone altogether. I'm sure other factors played a part in why this happened—stress, for instance—but I believe that if I could've used my hands as much as I needed to, I would've been able to continue producing milk. So it was par for the course that I felt deep guilt and shame about choosing the comfort of my therapy gloves over the extreme discomfort of breastfeeding. Why didn't I just take the gloves off when I was feeding her and deal with the pain for a little while? Wouldn't it have been worth it? I've asked myself these questions many times and have been harder on myself than any mother should ever be.

Guilt is not just reserved for mothers who feel it toward themselves—it is also used by mothers who wield it against other mothers. There is a mantra in the parenting world, "Fed is best." This means as long as a baby is getting nutrients it doesn't matter what source they're coming from. But the truth is that most people silently judge a mother's choices and would really rather say, "*Breast*fed is the *only* best." Factually, this is true—breast milk remains the best source of nutrition for a newborn—but what about mothers with conditions or disabilities, such as those who suffer from chronic pain or whose bodies don't make enough milk?

Flogging women with judgment over their choices as mothers serves no purpose other than to

further discredit us and the innate intelligence of
our instinct. To judge the choices of new mothers is
to say you do not trust their instinct and to not trust
a woman's instinct is to devalue our most primitive
form of intelligence. I've done it myself, catching the
words as they slip out of my mouth when I'm telling a
new mom friend how she should or shouldn't get her
baby to nap in a way that points out what she's doing
is wrong instead of what a possible solution might
be. There is no respected space in modern society
for women to decide, live, and nurture among themselves outright, *without* judgment. So we return
to the more familiar, accepted understanding of
women, the one that paints us archetypically as untrustworthy. This is how most women have learned
to behave toward one another, to question and doubt
one another's most primal decisions in the form of
disguised sisterly support. Instead of sharing wisdom and nonjudgmental advice, women for the most
part have taught one another to see what each of us
is doing wrong rather than what we are doing right.
Women who do not wish to have children or to get
married are made to feel like failures simply for not
choosing the path historically reserved for them;
queer women who choose to have children are judged
for their choices in how they conceive, adopt, or pur-
sue surrogacy; and transgender women's choices
barely even exist yet, including basic access to repro-

ductive health care. There are conservative women who benefit from and uphold male-dominated power structures that do not benefit their fellow women. There are liberal women who chastise other liberal women for not being liberal enough. There are feminists who dictate to other feminists what the definition of feminism should be, feminists who shame women for not identifying as feminists, and women who trash those who do identify as feminists. There are women who do not believe other women's accounts of sexual violence, women who ally with men at any cost, women who belittle civil rights movements formed by other women because they do not align with their style of activism, women who say they won't vote for other women just because of their gender.

No woman escapes the judgment paradigm, which is often used to gauge Western culture's true feelings on whether or not women can or should be trusted. And the question of whether women's instincts can or should be trusted is directly tied to the question of whether women can or should be trusted with larger forms of power. If we see women as not knowing what's truly "best" for their children, then we can also see women as not knowing what's truly best for the board, for the company, or for the country.

I had to learn to trust my instincts and to be kind to myself in the face of a world that had not been kind to me. After Marlow was born, I slept as much as I could and took up meditation. I stopped caring about losing all the weight I'd gained from pregnancy and instead went on a healthy, anti-inflammatory diet for a month. I worked hard to restrain my worrying, to rein in the anxieties of work or about the way I looked and what was expected of me post-birth. I enjoyed time with my daughter, uninterrupted by patterns of self-defeating thought (for the most part). I understood that many of these things were real privileges that not all working mothers could gift themselves, so I didn't squander them anymore. I didn't waste my self-care on fear.

We are taught so little about the health and safety of our physical bodies and also so little about how to protect them. Women have been kept in the dark of our own light, having to go to extraordinary lengths to educate others about what we need, from our basic rights to affordable health care, to our own sexual pleasures, to our emotional well-being. The burden is on women to be self-taught in a world where most men are already self-made—the latter being defined by expectations, the former by limitations.

I believe that our culture's practice of constantly questioning women's instinctual intelligence has made room for great abuse against the bodies that house that instinct. It is easier to abuse the female body when the instinct of that body is discredited. Women must be allowed to better care for their physical selves and protect other women's abilities to do the same at all costs, including the right to feel what they need to feel, openly and without shame, and to heal at the pace their bodies need to heal, without blame.

12

As a child actress, I used to be known for being able to cry on cue. It was something that came naturally to me, something I was very good at. Adults would applaud me for this gift of mine—the gift of forced emoting. I even had a running joke with directors: Just tell me which cheek you want the tear on and how far down you want it to fall and I'll make it happen. Everyone had always been so impressed by this immeasurable skill. When TV shows aired or films came out in which I had a crying scene, neighbors and friends alike would tell my parents how amazing I was, how talented, and how lucky they were to have me as their talented daughter.

When you're a child, all you want to do is please adults, to make them happy and proud of you. So the better an actress I was, the more I could get hired, and the more I could get hired, the more I would be praised and, ultimately, seen. This is how I learned how to be loved. Not only by my parents, but by everyone.

I have often wondered about the side effects and damage caused to the central nervous system by forcibly emoting for a living, especially during an age when the body is still growing. The brain and its more than 100 billion neurons coupled with the spinal cord and its access to the body's organs and thousands of nerves form the central nervous system, a main control center where everything is weighed and decided. The central nervous system has three main functions: to collect sensory information from its surroundings, to process that information and interpret it, and then to respond. Your central nervous system begins forming in utero, as early as five weeks old, and is pretty much responsible for all the ways in which you receive and give in this world, emotionally and otherwise. It is an intrinsically complex system starting from the rudiment of the neural tube at the base of your skull and spreading all throughout your body.

So what happens when any person, not just a child actor like me, lives a life dependent on overuse and unintended abuse of their central nervous system? I think about the survivors of abusive men such as Harvey Weinstein or Bill Cosby. Some of these women I am lucky to call my friends. They have suffered from long-term harassment, psychological threat, and even exile from a society that didn't believe them until women began sharing their stories of sexual violence en masse at the end of 2017. It has taken its toll not only on their minds and careers, but on their nervous systems, too. Some of these women have suffered from severe psychotic breaks, suicidal ideation, depression, and more. But some of them have issues symptomatic of a chronically fatigued central nervous system—symptoms such as autoimmune diseases, blood-flow disruptions, degeneration of nerves and tissue, or structural defects.

A friend of mine recently went through a very public court battle with a man she accused of sexually assaulting her. She told me all kinds of strange, undiagnosable ailments have come up since the prolonged court case began. She knew that the act of sexual violence itself took part of her life away from her, but everything that happened subsequently—her bank accounts drained from paying lawyers, the loss of friendships, and the emotional costs of the intimidation practices her assailant used—took part of her body away from her, too. Now her body is in a perpetual state of damage control, and she has to make sure nothing gets too stressful or else she has a "flare-up" in which the nerves in her body start tingling, burning, and going numb.

Sound familiar?

Typically, central nervous system disorders occur due to substance abuse, vascular disorders, exposure to toxins, or various forms of injuries, but I'd make the case that overexposure to emotional duress can be equally damaging—whether that emotion is being overused or suppressed. So many of the physical ailments I began to feel in my early thirties seemed like scarring from my own central nervous system's misuse as a child actor. I spent more than a decade telling my body that its mother had died and so it should cry, that it was a tough cop who liked to beat people up so it should be enraged, that it was being dragged out of an elevator by a serial killer so it should be terrified, that it was a crippled corpse rotting in a bedroom closet so it should be broken, that it was a dead body floating in a lake so it should feel nothing, that it was being raped so it should feel numb.

After I gave birth to my daughter and the inflammation left my body almost a year later, I still struggled with many issues pertaining to my nervous system. What was most revealing was that these issues arose only after I decided to take a break from acting—only after my own Era of Ignition had begun. It was only then, in the permission of that self-reflection, that my body began to show signs of its wreckage. I could feel the physical effects of my long-term programming, like aftershocks of my career's earthquake. And I have spent years undoing those tremors. I work hard at being kind to myself and honest about what I feel so as to never confuse or lie to my body again. I do not always succeed. But I do try.

The trauma of a difficult postpartum healing triggered a painful, not-so-distant memory of the other time my body had gone through something like this—the termination of my earlier pregnancy. The realization of the similarities between the two experiences took my breath away, and I was suddenly thrust back into the memory of the weeks I spent in my body after I had the abortion. I remembered physically soothing my body and telling it that everything was going to be okay. I would physically touch the parts of it where damage had been caused: my abdomen, my chest, my heart. I told my body, out loud, that I loved it and knew it was confused but that we would get through this together.

Reconnecting with our bodies in this way can help reconnect us with the pain of much older wounds—the wounds of childhood, which will someday, if not processed, become the wounded inner child harming our adult lives. By making myself aware of my adult body's pain through touch, talk, and psychological work, I was able to soothe it and reconnect with it in a way that I hadn't been able to do since early childhood. In the same way a young child discovers they have feet and a belly button and fingers and can run for the first time, I was rediscovering those parts of my body that I felt I had abandoned or neglected for so long. And in that soothing, I was able to connect with a deeper voice inside me: the voice of that lost and abandoned girl who left her childhood to become a full-time professional actress—the girl who gave herself away to the duties of adulthood before she even knew who she was.

My therapist, Evan, used to make me carry around a picture of myself as a little girl from a time when I had no worries, no adult responsibilities—from an age when I felt free. The picture I chose was one I found in my mom's scrapbook of me at four years old, riding a rocking horse in my parents' living room, an explosive laugh spread across my face and my hair caught in mid-whip. In that picture's moment, there was no grown-up responsibility, nothing but innocent joy in my life. I was young, I was happy, I had no obligations or resentments. I clipped the photo in my dream journal and carried it around with me for years, visually reconnecting with the girl in that picture and releasing myself from the feeling of having a life stolen from me before I was capable of making my own decisions.

In my mom's scrapbook, I also found an old newsletter that I'd written for my fan club when I was twelve years old. The title? "Hollywood Is Hard." The voice of the letter's pre-teen author is that of a hopeful young girl filled with equal parts naiveté and wisdom. Its themes read like premonitions of a life I would forever struggle to define—themes of isolation, objectification, frustration; a dismantled childhood. As I read the letter now, I am stirred by what I see: a child beginning to comprehend how unfair and lonely her journey will be, and also a child projecting confidence as a means of survival, telling herself what she needs to tell herself in order to live. Most of all, I see a child who so desperately wants to be seen. *Really* seen. Not as a glittery object of pop culture idolatry, but as a truth-teller, a straight-shooter, and, most important, a storyteller. I see a child who is an artist, beyond the career of acting. A child with the deep, psychic knowledge to write her own foreshadowing, to say in that newsletter: "I want to be a writer someday." This was a desire that would eventually become my truth. And my maternal instinct is to protect the girl who wrote those words. To reach through the twenty-five-year-old crumpled pages of that newsletter and tell her something that will help her get through it all. To help ease her into the world and let her know it won't be easy, but she *will* find her way. She *will* be heard. She *will* be seen.

This will be you, I want to show her. *This will be you in the form of a blazing fire.*

SOMETIMES I CATCH MYSELF leaning harder into stressful environments as an unhealthy way of reconnecting with that old trauma because in a way, it's all I've ever known. The entertainment business has created in me a Stockholm syndrome that tells me I will only ever feel comfortable when existing back in that old place of emotional chaos and stress. Social media and most especially Twitter are prime examples of places that bring back those old patterns, and often I will find myself logging on even when I know I shouldn't—even when I know it will fill me with dread, extreme anxiety, or unnecessary stress. But those feelings have been the foundation on which I have built my infrastructure, so they are familiar to me, and in that familiarity, I find ease in returning to them, however toxic they sometimes are. That's why it's so important for us to create better boundaries with environments that can cause our bodies to fall back into recognizable relapses and why it's so necessary to keep doing the work to literally rewire our brains so that they have options when they go into fight mode—not just the one protective option of self-sabotage and shutting down. As my dear friend Amy Poehler says, "It's important to create your own austerities before life does it for you in a mean-ass way." Preach, Poehler. By "austerities," she means new patterns of healthy behavior, ways of standing firmly for what you believe in and not letting people steer your moral compass for you. And that "mean-ass way" usually reveals itself in the body by taking control when we will not, a power struggle between the mind and the body that can come with some serious repercussions. We have to learn to create boundaries for ourselves. To step back from people and spaces that harm us, whether they intend to or not. Because what we absorb affects the functionality of our physicality. And we must take the best care of every part of us, especially now, in this time of existential wildfires.

Because this world needs you. I need you.

13

"Dad, I need to ask you if you remember something," I said to my father over the phone one evening in the fall of 2017. I was calling him for a specific reason and he could sense the pointedness in my voice. "Do you remember . . . do you remember when I was a teenager and still driving my first car, and I went to Mel's Diner with Billy after seeing that band? Do you remember what happened that night?"

My father did remember. I didn't have to prompt him or jump-start his memory with hints in order for him to recount the time I came home from that diner and told him the actor James Woods had hit on us and asked if we wanted to go to Las Vegas with him that very evening. When I told Mr. Woods I was only sixteen, he said, "Even better."

It has always been incumbent on women to verify stories of abuse—sexual and otherwise—to a ludicrously impossible degree. We must provide copious amounts of evidence pertaining to an accusation in order to have a fraction of the respect instantly and without question afforded to the accused. It's not enough to simply just *say* an abuse happened; survivors must also prove they have the receipts of said abuse, ad nauseam, ad infinitum, by providing witnesses, alibis, texts, photographic evidence, good character, a clean record, no history of mental illness or substance abuse. They must be intelligent, graceful, eloquent, and never perceived as asking for it. Survivors must also be attractive enough, the correct weight, and the right gender in order for people to believe anyone would even *want* to assault or harass them in the first place, let alone actually do it. They must have no priors—from felonies to outspokenness to sexual prowess and freedom.

In the judicial world, lawyers refer to a sexual assault survivor who passes all these outlandish tests as "the perfect victim." Most district attorneys and prosecutors will not actively seek to press charges against a perpetrator unless a fail-safe survivor has made said accusations—their defendant must be morally, physically, and characteristically impeccable. Almost 90 percent of cases are successfully acquitted under this model of attack by a defense team, and victims, perfect or otherwise, are left to pick up the broken pieces of their lives, shattered on the courtroom floor for everyone to see.

Which is why my first instinct after accusing James Woods of hitting on me when I was sixteen years old was to call my father and see if he remembered me telling him about it after it happened. I began to create a mental checkmate checklist, a corroboration that would ensure my story would be taken seriously.

A few days before, I had seen a tweet from my old friend, the actor Armie Hammer. Armie and I had shot a film in Spain and spent the better part of two months locked in an elevator together during the shoot. Needless to say, we had been through a lot together and had become friends. From what I could tell, James Woods had made a judgmental comment on Twitter regarding Armie's film *Call Me by Your Name,* in which his twenty-four-year-old character dates a seventeen-year-old. Mr. Woods condemned the idea of dating anyone underage. Armie responded by calling him a hypocrite, pointing out that Mr. Woods was known for dating extremely young women. My cheek twitched. I paused. I reread the tweet. And the memory was instantly triggered. I didn't think long about it before replying to the thread by telling Armie, and the world, my story, unaware that I had just opened a box of matches above an impending inferno.

Media outlets across the world picked up on the

story and soon Mr. Woods had given a statement to
The Hollywood Reporter calling my story a lie—calling
me a liar. I stared at the word as it hung in my head
like a knife taunting its old scar. *Liar.* Every cell of
my blood growled. My history—the history of my
deniability—opened like a book paged with razor
blades, sharp and dangerous, and my entire body
flooded with a ferociousness I had often felt but
never fully acted on.

My response was to publish a letter in *Teen Vogue,*
proclaiming a form of war against him—against any
and all men like him. "I see your gaslight and now
will raise you a scorched earth," I wrote. The next
day, I texted my friend Roxane Gay and told her I
wanted to write a piece on the chronic disbelief of
women and their stories in society, and I asked if she
would feel comfortable putting me in touch with her
editor at the *New York Times.* She made the connection, and a week later my op-ed, "I'm Done With Not
Being Believed," was published in the Sunday paper.
I lit the match and chucked it into a kindling world.

In addition to recounting my experience with
James Woods, I cited another incident I experienced
as a young actress in Hollywood:

When I was twenty-one, I went into the office of a
producer of the television show I was starring in
to discuss a big problem. By this point I had been
acting for more than a decade, and the show was

very successful and beloved. Still, I was nervous about facing the firing squad of Emmys that sat behind him and saying what I had to say.

A crew member had kept showing up to my apartment after work unannounced, going into my trailer while I wasn't in it, and staring daggers at me from across the set. I liked him at first. He was very sweet and kind in the beginning. We flirted a bit on set. But I was in a relationship. And liking someone certainly didn't merit the kind of behavior he was exhibiting, which was making me feel unsafe.

My hands were freezing and I balled my wardrobe skirt up around my fists as I spoke. It was all caught in my throat—my embarrassment that it had gotten to this point. The producer listened. Then he said, "Well, there are two sides to every story."

For women in America who come forward with stories of harassment, abuse and sexual assault, there are not two sides to every story, however noble that principle might seem. Women do not get to have a side. They get to have an interrogation. Too often, they are questioned mercilessly about whether their side is legitimate. Especially if that side happens to accuse a man of stature, then that woman has to consider the scrutiny and repercussions she'll be subjected to by sharing her side.

Every day, women across the country consider the risks. That is our day job and our night shift. We have a diploma in risk consideration. Consider that skirt. Consider that dark alley. Consider questioning your boss. Consider what your daughter will think of you. Consider what your mother will think of what your daughter will think of you. Consider how it will be twisted and used against you in a court of law. Consider whether you did, perhaps, really ask for it. Consider your weight. Consider dieting. Consider agelessness. Consider silence.

It's no wonder that the United States Bureau of Justice Statistics reported that from 2006 to 2010, 65 percent of sexual assaults went unreported. What's the point if you won't be believed?

The emotional cost alone of bringing up such memories publicly or coming forward with such recollections is pure bankruptcy. It is spiritual foreclosure.

I have been afraid of speaking out or asking things of men in positions of power for years. What I have experienced as an actress working in a business whose business is to objectify women is frightening. It is the deep end of a pool where I cannot swim. It is a famous man telling you that you are a liar for what you have remembered. For what you *must* have misremembered, unless you have proof. The women I know, myself included, are done, though, playing the credentials game. We are learning that the more we open our mouths, the more we become a choir. And the more we are a choir, the more the tune is forced to change.

What I wrote became one of the most widely read and shared opinion pieces in the *New York Times* in 2017. On the evening of the day it was published, I accompanied my husband, David, to a pre–Emmy Awards party that Jeffrey Katzenberg throws every year. I was not prepared for the conversations I would have that night with those who had read the piece that morning, which seemed to be virtually everyone. The head of development for one of the largest television networks saw me from across the room and approached me quickly. She took my hands in hers and told me how she had been sexually harassed and then assaulted during her time as an intern at a network when she was younger. My article had brought up so much old, buried pain for her, but it also made her cheer out loud. It made her feel seen for the first time in a long time, she told me. Later, a well-known and beloved actress told me a story about being groped by her male costar on multiple occasions and said that reading the piece helped her come to the decision to finally report him.

A bartender told me a story about being fired from a recent job for reporting her boss's sexual advances. Another woman, walking around the party serving hors d'oeuvres on a tray, said to me, "If I wasn't holding this plate I'd probably ask to hug you. But then I'd probably burst into tears so maybe it's all for the best." Two wives of network presidents—one a schoolteacher and the other a stay-at-home mom—simply whispered, "Thank you," while their husbands stood nearby, talking shop. A man working at the valet pulled our car up and told me his girlfriend had made him read the piece. "Powerful stuff," he said. "Made me think about some things." An otherwise uneventful evening celebrating Hollywood had turned into a charged spark of catharsis, en masse.

The impulse to defend my credibility publicly against a man with a predatory past was more than just a breaking point; it was a breakthrough. It was a combustion of cumulative injustices experienced throughout my life, because it wasn't just James Woods I was fed up with; it was all the James Woodses who came before him—from bosses to ex-boyfriends. After attending that party and speaking to all of those women from different walks of life, it was clear I wasn't the only one fed up with being talked down to, talked at, dismissed, silenced, ignored, and shut out of rooms, conversations, and creative power.

The stories shared with me over the following week, from women across job titles, races, and socioeconomic backgrounds, were life changing. No—life *igniting*. I could feel our collective unconscious seething with ammunition, preparing to unload centuries' worth of wrongdoing. A new kind of silence-resistant rage was percolating in women I knew and women I didn't; it was in the tone of female journalists, in women running for office, in my very own mother, who told me over the phone, "Our grandmothers are with us now, Amber Rose. Trump and his squad of rapists and racists have risen the dead. He messed with the wrong army of ghosts." Even old stories of predators whose assaults had merely flamed indignation but never resulted in repercussion—Woody Allen and Roman Polanski, for instance—were boiling up again with a fresh furnace of palpable force from women. Women who, very much like me, were done with not being believed.

A few days after the publication of that piece in September, Lena Dunham texted me to tell me an investigative reporter for the *New York Times* by the name of Jodi Kantor had read my piece and wanted to contact me about a story she was working on. Coincidentally, that very same evening, I went to dinner with a friend at a restaurant in Los Angeles and someone tapped me on the shoulder while seated at the bar. I turned around and a man introduced himself to me as Ronan Farrow. He had also read the piece I wrote and wanted to talk about a story he had been working on for more than nine months, "involving one of the most powerful producers in your business."

"Do you mean *the* most powerful producer?" I asked him.

"Yes. That one."

Over the next several weeks, I quietly and carefully reached out to people in Hollywood who might
want to go on the record regarding the man at the
center of both reporters' investigations: Harvey
Weinstein. Out of more than a dozen people I spoke
to, I'm aware of only one who was willing to speak to
Ms. Kantor. I reached out to various powerful women
and men across job titles—from publicists to agents
to movie stars—and none of them wanted to speak
to a reporter on the record about Mr. Weinstein.
"What's the point?" an actress friend said to me
when I asked her if she wanted to talk to Jodi regarding an incident she once had with Weinstein in an
elevator. "No one's ever going to be able to stop him.
He's been doing this forever. He got away with it then
and he'll get away with it again. He'll sue the *Times*
into silence. And what will happen to those of us who
spoke up? Our careers and lives will be burned at the
stakes while Harvey pours on the gasoline."

She wasn't wrong. For more than a century, such
fuels had found their flame using the tinder of bad
men and the women who allied with them. The world
watched as Anita Hill was discredited when she testified to being sexually harassed by Clarence Thomas,
a powerful federal judge who was aiming to become a
Supreme Court justice in 1991, only to watch the exact
same narrative play out in a strikingly similar way
almost thirty years later with Christine Blasey Ford

testifying against Supreme Court nominee Brett Kavanaugh. Had we learned nothing? We clearly hadn't.

In both cases, but most especially the Kavanaugh case, the female accusers gave testimonies with extremely reserved emotion while their hands shook and they bit back tears. The accused male judges, Thomas and especially Kavanaugh, did as they pleased, emotionally and otherwise; they yelled and flailed their hands, and ran wild with their emotions and language. Both men were outraged and offended, treating the mere fact that they had to testify as assaults on their good names. Kavanaugh in particular was so upset he was practically spitting on the microphone while he yelled about how his name had been tarnished, and he broke down crying on more than one occasion. If a woman had ever dared to show emotion in the way that Kavanaugh did, she would have been immediately deemed erratic, unstable, and unfit for office. Kavanaugh's emotional outburst rendered him human in the eyes of the almost entirely white male Senate Judiciary Committee panel, whereas Dr. Blasey Ford's testimony was met with eye-rolling from Republican committee chair Senator Chuck Grassley and with complete silent disinterest from every Republican on the panel. What my actress friend had said about Weinstein was very true and felt like a premonition of things to come: Men get away with these types of egregious behaviors and go on living as if nothing ever happened. The entitled frat boys of the world are shown that sexually terrorizing women in their youth comes with little to no consequences. It is behavior that is grossly rewarded by teaching them nothing and allowing them to grow up into powerful men—into movie moguls, presidents of television networks, and chairs of boards—who continue with the same behavior, unchecked.

But something was shifting with this investigation of Harvey Weinstein; something was different this time. It was about more than just being enraged—women have always been angered by their circumstances; that is nothing new. This time our rage was propelled into movement, a reaction so strong we didn't even pause to ask for the nation's permission. What was once a silent and isolating daily exercise in how to tolerate marginalization was turning into a collective eruption of vocalized grievances. Women across the country didn't even have to talk to one another in order to feel the shaking. To see the birds fleeing from the trees. To know a colossal wave of change was coming.

"Sit tight" began a text message to me from Jodi Kantor on the evening of October 4, 2017, the night before her story on Weinstein broke in the *New York Times.* "The women are going to need support for telling their stories. You will know exactly what to do."

14

I was the seasoned soap opera starlet, the incidental
ingénue, the accidental adolescent actress turned
adult apparition, haunting her own future by existing only in her past. I was the famous one, known for
being unknown. I was an ideological in-between, a
neither here nor there artist, taken seriously by few
outside of the poetry community, and even fewer
within it. I was the girl who was a blind spot in the
mirrors of powerful men. The girl called upon to
help rewrite, workshop, or give notes on scripts by
men as an assumed favor, only to never be hired by
them or to receive any credit. I was the secret weapon
for everyone else's arsenals but my own. I was the girl
lost amid privilege and invisibility, forever seen as

what I used to be, not who I am. That was me. *That was me in the form of fading fire.*

And then, that girl, that starlet, that in-between, that some-bodied nobody, that fading fire—was extinguished. The woman who emerged was done not just with not being believed, but also with not being listened to, taken seriously, heard, seen, counted, or chosen for the job. She was done with doing for others—of being a Cyrano for male cisness, consistently asked by peers in positions of power to help them remain there without any reciprocity or consideration given. I was done with selling myself short so that men could buy themselves success. And if someone with the access, privilege, and reach that I grew up with was feeling this way, I could only imagine what less-well-connected members of the even more greatly underrepresented communities in my industry were feeling.

What has been reborn in me is being reborn in every woman across the country. My Saturn Return—my soul's dizzying upheaval, my identity's eruption, my trajectory's crisis, my raw dawning—was mirroring the country's Saturn Return and its own dizzying upheaval, its identity's eruption, its trajectory's crisis, its raw dawning. We are a nation that is morally backpedaling, scared of change, and stuck in the back pocket of social media's isolation and alienation. We are a nation that not only refuses to resolve matters face-to-face, we refuse to see eye-to-eye. We're not only lost, we're just now coming to terms with the fact that we've always *been* lost. And finding ourselves and others will take more than just strength. It will take stamina. This is the age of action, this Era of Ignition; we are a collective cognition's fired-up engine, revving into revelation, unsure of where we're going but knowing we can no longer stay where we have been.

In October 2017, the *New York Times* published a blistering report of several women who had been sexually assaulted or harassed by the movie mogul Harvey Weinstein. Shortly after that, an even more damning article by Ronan Farrow was published in *The New Yorker,* complete with an audiotape of Weinstein pressuring a young actress named Ambra Battilana Gutierrez into going up to a hotel room with him. "Don't embarrass me," you could hear him warning Gutierrez on the tape. "Please. I'm not gonna do anything. I swear on my children. Please come in. On everything. I'm a famous guy."

I was sitting in my car in traffic on the George Washington Bridge while my husband drove and our nine-month-old daughter hummed "Twinkle, Twinkle, Little Star" in the backseat. *I swear on my children.* His words echoed in my head. The words made me sick to my stomach. "Jesus," my husband said as he drove, "what a monster."

"This is what we're up against every single day," I said to him. "This kind of coercion and just . . . blind greed."

"Well, not all of them are this bad, I hope. This guy is fucking terrible."

"Yes, many of them are this bad in their own right. In their arrogance, in their petulance. This is how these guys act, whether it's about sex or not."

It took a moment for women—especially actresses and powerful women within the entertainment business—to respond to the article and condemn Weinstein's actions. Hollywood was like a massive herd of deer in the biggest set of headlights we had ever known, completely frozen with equal parts fear, shock, and, of course, complicity. Kantor's words beat down the doors in my head: *These women are going to need support.* So the moment I read the stories and heard the audiotape, I logged on to Twitter and began to compose a tweet condemning Harvey Weinstein, my hands trembling and my mouth dry with fear. I was one of a very small handful outside of the accusers themselves coming out to condemn him, and the action felt like being one of the first ones to taste the soup in order to find out whether or not it was poisoned and could kill you.

It is important to remember that while most of us were seething, we were also truly terrified. I know composing a tweet doesn't seem like a big deal, but in this case it was. There was no way of knowing how the story about Weinstein was going to play out, and the terror of a powerful man's retaliation kept actresses in a momentary state of shocked suspension. Questions gathered in my mind, as I'm sure they did in others': What if I say something and his career survives this allegation? What if I am blacklisted and I never work again? What if I am harassed, stalked, and willfully silenced—all real experiences that were revealed to have happened to the likes of Rose McGowan when Harvey Weinstein hired ex-Mossad agents to torment her? And what if all of this happens and no one has my back, because they too are fearful of the same thing happening to them? All of my questions led to the same truth, which is that if I didn't say something—if we didn't all just take the risk and say something—we would never break the cycle of abuse. We would forever be stuck in a pattern of watching it happen to someone else and being afraid that it may someday happen to us. So I took to Twitter and publicly condemned him, mere minutes after *The New Yorker* story broke.

There was a lot of blame thrown around on social media in those subsequent days, and one of the first groups of people to be accused of not supporting the women who came forward were those actresses in silent states of suspended shock. This, to me, was incredibly unfair. Why was it the responsibility of other women—women who very likely had been threatened and abused in the exact same manner as the women in the article—to speak up first? We too have endured hell and it's not something you just snap out of instantly.

A deeply unsettling narrative was taking shape that questioned why everyone in the entertainment business was acting so shocked when they all knew what Weinstein had done. But this narrative was untrue. It is very likely that many people knew he was not just a harasser but a rapist. But a lot of people, myself included, had only ever heard rumors that amounted to your uncle's creepy friend whose hand would rest too low on your back when hugging you. I believe many actresses were shielded from such information so as to protect those people who were in the pockets of Harvey Weinstein, or who wanted to be.

I myself never knew this information about him. The only interaction I had ever had with him was five years ago, as I stood with a producer and financier friend of mine, Megan Ellison, at a party at the Chateau Marmont while he tried to pressure her into co-financing a film with him. In retrospect, his entreaties remind me so much of that same man on the audiotape—a man who wouldn't take no for an answer. "Believe me, you're not going to want to miss out on a deal like this. Once these types of girls pop, you can make a lot of money off of them," he said in reference to the actress Jennifer Lawrence, who had just been nominated for an Oscar, as if she was a prized hound he had purchased at a dog show. Megan tried to change the subject by introducing him to me. He made no acknowledgment of my presence, not a look, let alone a hello, and continued badgering Megan.

Every woman who was a part of the journey that followed in the wake of Harvey Weinstein's comeuppance has her own version of how everything unfolded in the subsequent months—her own version based on what she saw, who she confided in, who she was empowered by, and how she found her fire and turned it into action. This is my version of what happened based on what I experienced. I was but one voice among the many, ready to do something big and make it count.

DAYS AFTER THE LATEST WAVE of the #MeToo movement—originally founded by activist Tarana Burke some two decades earlier—broke wide open at the end of 2017 and flooded social media with widespread stories of sexual violence and harassment across the country, I texted Megan and said I wanted to get a group of women together at her office to talk candidly about what was going on in our industry. Megan is currently the owner of the only woman-owned, -financed, and -run film and television studio in Hollywood, called Annapurna Pictures. She is an icon and inspiration in the film business but also, sadly, an anomaly. I wasn't sure of the goal of the meeting I was proposing just yet, but I felt compelled to stay as close as possible to the women in my field of work while this tectonic shift was happening all around us.

Megan and I created a list of some of the most powerful voices in entertainment and invited them to come to her office for an informal, off-the-record, safe conversation. More than twenty women from across the industry attended, from Roxane Gay to America Ferrera to Jill Soloway to Tig Notaro. The room was set up so that we were sitting in a circle around a large table, facing one another and facing what we had never dared to before.

The meeting proved complex, cathartic, uncomfortable, and challenging. We were in uncharted territory, giving ourselves permission to have big, authoritative, and decisive discussions about the future without a single man present to give us his big, authoritative, and decisive opinion on our future. Without that voice in the room, the air felt heavy with a sort of PTMD: post-traumatic misogyny disorder. The questions lingered in my head and likely in the heads of the other women sitting there, too: How do we begin? What can we say? What should we not say? Who will go first? Are we allowed to?

We were there to talk about the inequality and power imbalance mostly between men and women, but another issue presented itself, one that, up until recently, had never been at the forefront of feminist conversation: the inequality and power imbalance among women themselves, white and otherwise. While white women have certainly been kept out of creative rooms and conversations throughout the history of the entertainment business, women of color, LGBTQIA women, and women with disabilities were never even let into the building to begin with.

A 2018 study from the Annenberg Institute's Annenberg Inclusion Initiative found damning evidence of just how underrepresented some kinds of women still are in Hollywood. The study looked at the top 100 films per year over the course of a decade, from 2007 to 2017—eleven hundred films in total—and found that only forty-three of them were directed by women (roughly 7 percent of all films in the study), and that only three of those were Asian American women and four were black women. Only 2.5 percent of characters depicted over that decade were women with disabilities. All in all, only twenty-one of the lead actors out of the top-grossing one hundred films in 2017 were played by minorities. And of those twenty-one underrepresented actors, only four were women of color.

These underrepresented minorities of women have largely been left out both in front of and behind the camera for generations in the entertainment business, not just by men in positions of power, but by those few white women in positions of power, too.

This imbalance was evident in the meeting that day, with the participants overwhelmingly consisting of cis white women, a fact many such women had never before had to think about or hold themselves accountable for. But there in the room, devoid of men, facing one another literally and metaphorically, it could not be unseen. As one black woman at the table put it when we began to set an intention for the meeting, "I'm looking forward to seeing how women of color will be included in this space today and not left out, as we usually are."

During the meeting, America Ferrera brought to our attention a stunning letter that had recently been published by the Alianza Nacional de Campesinas and signed by more than 700,000 women farmworkers, standing in solidarity with the women in the entertainment business. "We wish that we could say we are shocked to learn that this is such a pervasive problem in your industry," America quoted as she read the letter out loud to us. "Sadly, we're not surprised because it's a reality we know far too well. Countless farmworker women across our country suffer in silence because of the widespread sexual harassment and assault that they face at work . . ."

The letter went on to demand respect, accountability, and real change for all of womankind, not just for farmworkers. America, along with producer Dede Gardner, came up with the idea of a response letter, one that, as America said in the room, "Must be something that is tied to an action." She was right. It needed a tether; otherwise it would be nothing more than a symbolic gesture. We needed to stand with the female farmworkers in a tangible way, one that would send a message to the world and put it on notice.

After the meeting commenced, I learned of another meeting that was happening across town. It seemed Megan and I were not the only women with the idea to get in a room together and talk about what we had never dared to before. From what I heard, meetings were forming all over Los Angeles. Women, from agents to managers to screenwriters to studio executives to assistants, were getting together with real aim and purpose to change our business from the inside out. This was, of course, the worst fear of men in positions of power throughout our industry—that women across titles, status, and representation would get together and start talking to one another candidly and without fear. "Once they know that you all *know*," a male executive told me one night over drinks during this time, "it's over. Their dominance is lost forever. And they know it."

America invited me to join her at a second meeting, which was taking place in a gated community at an actress's home. While the meeting with Megan aimed to discuss larger systemic problems within the entertainment business, this second meeting was for actresses alone to discuss the experiences that pertained specifically to our line of work. When I arrived at the house, roughly a dozen women of different ages, races, and statures were sitting in the living room holding Post-its, Sharpies, notebooks, and computers. A giant poster board leaned against an easel and a mind map of bubbled thoughts, comments, and inspired ideas spread across the wide paper. From across the room, I couldn't make out much of it, but the words in one larger bubble jumped out and grabbed hold of me when I read them: Sisters in Solidarity.

Someone handed me a pad of paper and a pen. I jumped right in.

It is hard to know what solidarity looks like in an industry that perpetuates a feast-or-famine mentality and often pits women against one another. Yes, it is true that the industry is very competitive, but competition implies there is room for people to compete in the first place, and the fact remains for women, particularly minority women, there is no such room. We have never had real, public solidarity before, especially among women from different incomes and standings in the entertainment business. Up until that night, I had never in my two-and-a-half-decade career as an actress sat down with a group of my female peers with the specific purpose of discussing harassment, discrimination, inequality, and underrepresentation in our field. It was completely revolutionary.

We shared stories, career injustices, times we had been silenced or times when we couldn't find the strength to use our voices at all. We joked about the ridiculous beauty and weight standards we had all maintained in order for our careers to survive; then we got angry with our own obedient acceptance of the status quo. On more than one occasion, shock and grief gave way to tears, as we recalled the years' upon years' worth of eating disorders, blacklisting, and blackmail most of us had experienced.

I had spent my two decades as an actress being told how to mold myself to the business, not how to carve out a unique place for myself within it. Once when I was in my early twenties, my agent called to tell me how much the head of the studio that had just produced a big film I starred in loved me. He told her I had a very bright career ahead of me, if only I could tone up my body. Nicole Kidman was used as an example of the type of body I should consider achieving should I want to become a true star. My agent said, "You have a real choice right now with your career, Amber. If you can lose some weight and tone up your arms and body, this could be huge for you. You need to ask yourself the big question: Do you want to be a movie star or a character actress?"

I was five feet, seven inches tall and weighed 120.6 pounds. I remember this exact number so vividly because the day my agent called was the day I bought my first scale and weighed myself. I looked down at that number, which seemed to stare up at me accusingly, and I wondered what it would take to turn that 2 into a 1. It was the first time I weighed my creative worth and value based on my expected appearance.

It was not the first time I searched for my own self-worth in how I looked or how much I weighed, and it wouldn't be the last time either. I have lost movie roles for not being a desired size or sexual aesthetic and spent many years on sets being asked either directly or indirectly to "tone up," which is code for "lose weight." And if they were telling me this at 120 pounds and five-foot-seven, imagine how they were treating other women who might've weighed more than I did but who had perfectly normal, beautiful bodies, just like I had.

I recall one experience on a TV show where a male executive producer had mentioned to my agent that the network would like me to tone up a bit. I was so angry I spent weeks dieting and eating low carbohydrates and no bread just to prove to them how stupid they were and how quickly I could do it, as if it was no big request whatsoever. I dieted until my already flat, young stomach was even flatter and now hugging my ribs tightly. When the producer came on set, he saw me from across the room and pointed at my midriff and gave me a thumbs-up, like a well-meaning football coach. As if to say, "Look at you, tiger, out there starving yourself for the team! Go get 'em!" Later on he would say words that would stick in my head forever but take on new meaning as I got older: "I see you've been taking care of yourself nicely, Amber. Keep up the good work."

Extreme dieting and constant worry about the aesthetics of your body is not taking care of yourself, but women are taught from a very early age that it is. We see it in advertising, in the dolls we play with, and in the communities of women who raise us. It was modeled to me in a number of disheartening ways growing up: by watching the eating behaviors of other women on sets, by men in positions of authority who disguised such requests in the form of health advice and, even on occasion, from the mouth of my own father.

This is difficult for me to write about, but it's important to remember that even the men who are closest to us, who we love, are capable of being hurtful at times. When I was growing up, my father would often make comments about my weight or the way I looked. He would warn me that I am built like his mother and that if I was "not careful" I would end up like her. Meaning, fat. We have since had many very difficult conversations about the language he used with me back then, and he eventually got to a place where one of two things would happen when I would come to town to visit: If I wasn't thin, he wouldn't say anything about how I looked. But if I had lost weight, he would go out of his way to tell me how great I looked. He has since worked hard to stop talking to me like this and I'm proud of him for that, but it did take its toll on me when I was younger. I love my dad very much and can excuse this behavior as generational, but it's important that I am not silent about it. Silence isn't death. Silence is a deathly living.

I know that most men—especially men of my father's age, but not exclusive to it—mean well when they comment on a woman's size, shape, eating habits, or even clothing. Their intention is to give credit where their brain thinks credit is due: to a woman who has pleased the aesthetic standard they have been taught to believe is universally correct. All kinds of women have experienced conversations like this with family members who purport to love them unconditionally. Siblings and mothers can be complicit in this narrative as well, modeling truly unhealthy behavior of what, exactly, a woman should look like and worry about. A version of this would be watching any number of *The Real Housewives* television shows. I recall seeing an episode where one of the housewives takes her daughter to the doctor for a nose job consultation. I have watched this show with my own mother and felt swept up in the irony of it all. While I am lucky to have a mother who does not care about plastic surgery, I do have a mother who worries about how she looks in other ways. Like her, I too am an emotional eater, and at times a chronic dieter who is constantly trying to find the balance of health within the chaos of dieting trends. I know very few women who are not in the exact same boat with their mothers and with themselves.

I recognize that body shaming and dysmorphia are not reserved for women alone, and that many boys and men are taught to obsess over their bodies as well. But the difference is that their ability to get hired or be desired is not always dependent on how they look. Yes, sometimes this is true, like in the world of modeling, for instance, but overwhelmingly, severe ageism and sexism not only denies women the right to look how we want to look, but also denies us our livelihood in doing so, particularly in the entertainment industry. Only a small handful of talented actresses, women like Dame Judi Dench or Melissa McCarthy, have been able to look their age and be their own weight and still remain successful. The rest have had to stay in line or risk being thrown out of the club.

The only way to change this unrealistic beauty standard is for women to spend less time focused on our bodies and more time dismantling the system that upholds these cruel standards in the first place. Which is one of the many reasons why the meeting I attended with America that night was so powerful and freeing for me. I was in a room with women who were not only speaking about what we have been expected to do, but taking it one step further by saying: We are going to change it. And we are not asking for anyone's permission in doing so.

I left the meeting feeling a vortex of emotional volatility, bittersweet and blazing. These meetings with colleagues had halved me into equal parts extraordinary sadness and excruciating hope. One side said: *Why didn't we all do this sooner? What took us so long?* The other half said: *What took us so long still surrounds us, Amber. Go easy on yourself. We're going to have to fight like hell to get there.*

I drove toward the exit of the gated community on Sunset Boulevard only to find the main entrance gate was broken and wouldn't open. I got out of the car and tried to find a way to fix it. Another actress who had also been at the meeting pulled up and got out of her car to help me assess the situation.

"The gate's broken, we can't get out. We're stuck here until we die," I joked.

"Yeah, well, at least we're stuck together."

ON JANUARY 1, 2018, a letter in response to the women farmworkers, signed by me and more than three hundred of my peers in the entertainment business, was printed in the *New York Times*. "The struggle for women to break in, to rise up the ranks and to simply be heard and acknowledged in male-dominated workplaces must end," the letter read in part. "Time's up on this impenetrable monopoly."

The letter was the birth announcement for Time's Up, a movement born out of the mobilization of women at these many meetings, something we hoped to nurture into a fully operating organization. Spearheaded by America Ferrera and other women who had attended meetings from across industries—lawyers, activists, union presidents, and more—the letter was a quietly and carefully crafted endeavor months in the making. It was a labor of many loves—of longing for change, of loyalty to our communities, and of freedom's longevity. We spent every day making phone calls, asking women to sign the letter, ever careful not to let it leak, and setting up more meetings to continue what we had started.

But the most important part of this letter was that it followed through with what America had said that day in Megan's office—that it needed to be tied to action. During those months, a legal defense fund was being created by women I would come to work closely with over the course of the next year and call my friends—lawyer Robbie Kaplan; former chief of staff to Michelle Obama Tina Tchen; strategist and lawyer Hilary Rosen; director of the National Women's Law Center Fatima Goss Graves; along with female agents, managers, producers, directors, and actresses, such as Leslie Silva, Uzo Aduba, Sarah

AMBER TAMBLYN

Jessica Parker, Natalie Portman, and Jessica Chastain, among others. Many women who had been working to craft and shape the launch of Time's Up also made calls to friends, business partners, and peers, asking them to donate to the fund before it became public. Along with the publication of the letter, we were proud to announce we had raised $13 million for the Time's Up Legal Defense Fund, which has now exceeded more than $22 million in donations. The fund connects those who experience sexual misconduct, including assault, harassment, abuse, and related retaliation in the workplace or in trying to advance their careers, with legal and public relations assistance.

That entire first week of January, each of us spent countless hours to birth Time's Up into the world. We coordinated efforts on creating social media kits, outreach, language, follow-ups, and amplification. We strategized and theorized and bounced ideas off one another. We looked for what might be missing, might be unrepresented, might be harmful to other women. We used every ounce of our psychic energies, our instincts, and our widest peripheries. We were a syncing of storms, pissed off and in perfect rhythm. We were *angranized*—angry and organized. And even though we were exhausted from months of all-consuming work, the likes of which had become a full-time job, we were beaming with pride.

The work we had done often left us with little to no time to sleep, to see our families, or for other projects, but the labor of Time's Up was an undeniable and unforgettable declaration of our demands. And with it we had drawn an international line in the sand: You're either with women and the work we have set out to do or you're against us. You either want equal representation or you don't. You're either going to fight for the safety of all kinds of bodies and voices or you're not. You're either an arbiter of transformation or a harbinger of denigration. You're either a cog in the machine or the key in the ignition. You're either the ticking of the clock or you're the time that's up. Pick a side.

That night I went to my local bodega in Brooklyn, worn out yet beaming, and picked up a copy of the *New York Times*. I took it home, relieved David of baby monitor duties, and sat down on the couch with a glass of wine. I opened the paper to our letter, which filled the entire page. I texted America and asked her if she had picked up a copy yet. She wrote back quickly that she had and it had made her cry, which in turn made me cry. Sharing such a deeply profound moment in my history with this sister of mine—this Sister in Solidarity, this best friend of more than ten years, this beautiful thinker, teacher, and beacon of strength, this woman with whom I had been through so much—was something I will never forget.

On the monitor, my ten-month-old daughter slept on her back with her arms spread wide, her fingers twitching, embracing the room's darkness and the beginning flicker of an incoming dream, just as women everywhere were doing the same.

* * *

To learn more about and donate to the
Time's Up Legal Defense Fund, visit timesupnow.com.

15

What are Sisters in Solidarity? What does that mean exactly? Since that first meeting in Megan's office, the words of that black woman have stayed with me: *How will women of color be included in this space today and not left out, like we usually are?* It is something that should always be at the forefront of any feminist thinker's work, but often isn't.

Several years ago, I posted a picture of the women's suffrage movement on Instagram to honor the day in 1920 when all women in America finally got the right to vote. Until the Nineteenth Amendment was ratified, women were denied many of the same freedoms and rights that white men had always been afforded. I touted this as a sacred day for women and feminists, in particular, because it was an Era of Ignition for women of the early twentieth century.

But not for all women.

It was pointed out to me that while the ratification of the Nineteenth Amendment made it legal for all women and all African American people to vote (black men had gained the vote with the ratification of the Fifteenth Amendment forty years earlier, in 1870), that didn't mean that they actually *could*. Voter suppression and disenfranchisement were rampant during this time, most notably in Southern states and against African American communities, and especially against black women. White Southerners became extremely uneasy when black women registered to vote in large numbers (in some states, even more were registered than white women) and moved hell and earth in order to keep them from voting. Black men and women had to go through arbitrary, rigorous, and utterly ridiculous tests, such as reading and then interpreting the Constitution, in order to be considered worthy of voter registration. And even if they were able to pass these tests, they were then kept waiting in line for an entire day to get into a voting booth. White women, particularly affluent, upper-class white women, did not have this same problem. It wasn't until the years of Mary Church Terrell in the early-to-mid twentieth century, and the African American women's suffrage movement that followed in the 1960s, that women of color truly had such rights, more than forty years after the 1920 Amendment granting them the vote.

I was ashamed that I had never heard of the black women's suffrage movement. How is it possible that a feminist like me didn't know this? I went to a liberal arts school in Southern California when I was a kid; however, I never got an advanced degree. Was this something they taught in college? How was I in my early thirties and only hearing about this for the first time in my life?

There are many answers to this question: perhaps my history books did not cover this in class, or maybe it's because my liberal mother always told me to never see color and see everyone as equal. But at a certain point, these sound more like the excuses of a distant childhood, blaming how I was raised and educated rather than how I have continued to raise and educate myself as an adult woman. The true answer to how I could not have known about this significant historic milestone is actually quite simple: white feminism.

I am a white feminist. It has taken me years to own this pejorative term because I was afraid of how true it was, how true of *me*. But I own it because I do not want it to own me. The label is used to point out the glaringly inconsiderate and hypocritical allegiance white women have toward the ideals of feminism, but not to the actions behind them. I own this truth about myself and my white sisters, so I am not affronted when told by black women that my be-havior is that of a white feminist. I'm not affronted because it is important for me, and should be for all of us, to have accountability for what we have been given through what has been taken away from oth-ers. And responsibility, to me, is a deep interroga-tion of the many things I have been taught or have allowed myself to lazily accept. It is my responsibil-ity to *see* race. To see black and brown women for who they are, but to also see white women for who we are.

White women do not like to be called "white fem-inists" because we feel our long-term marginaliza-tion by white men somehow nullifies us from ever being accused or capable of doing the same thing to other women. Whether any white woman wants to admit this or not, it is true. And it is wrong.

One of the hardest hurdles for my fellow white women to get over has been our reactionary defen-siveness, like some unchecked involuntary muscle seizing up when we are taken to task for any num-ber of racist, disparaging, or inconsiderate ways in which we have ostracized black women. I know the thought of being called "racist" is many white people's worst fear, mine included, but we must dis-arm that fear and accept that we are guilty of doing or saying something racist almost daily, in the most nuanced of ways, whether we are aware of it or not.

This defensiveness is our very whiteness speak-ing on our behalf—a pathology of privilege that makes excuses rather than absorbs and learns. And when we are seen through and called out for this, the immediate reaction is one of self-preservation, to defend ourselves first and reflect last.

But what can we do to be better allies to women of different races, cultures, and socioeconomic backgrounds? First, we must acknowledge the long-standing foundational problems feminism has faced and then be really real with ourselves, and with one another, about how to fix them. And believe it or not, the fix is actually not that hard. It comes in the form of merely stepping aside and listening more than we talk. Which is exactly what we are asking men to do in this #MeToo moment.

So much of the ethos surrounding that first wave of (white) feminism still lives in all the subsequent waves that have followed—issues of power imbalance, erasure, and misappropriation that are not dissimilar to the problems white women face with men. But it is not the responsibility of black and brown women to excavate this problem for us, just as it is not women's responsibility to excavate problems for men. We must all do our own digging.

There are many ways in which we can be better allies and one of them is to pay attention to how, exactly, we define allyship. For generations, white women have centered themselves in conversations pertaining to representation and equality instead of amplifying voices that are far better suited—and, frankly, needed—to speak and be heard on the subject, especially now. We have linked arms to fight for equal rights with the sisters like us, in both race and class, but we have done little for those sisters of different races and classes who have been left behind. Part of our white defensiveness comes from the fact that we feel we *have* been great allies, so we don't think we deserve the title of white feminist. We have feminists like Gloria Steinem! And Alyssa Milano! We can point to a few good examples of intersectionality (a term coined by a black woman and leading scholar of critical race theory, Kimberlé Williams Crenshaw) as though these women speak for all of us.

What does being an ally mean to white women? Is it solidarity, or is it saviorship? Is it ceding the floor to black and brown voices, or just talking on their behalf about how the floor must be ceded? Is this not the very thing we accuse men of doing to us all the time? I encourage all of us to practice what we preach when fighting systems of power that have held us down, and to look hard and deep at how we have benefited from them and allowed them to remain intact by turning a blind eye.

I know about white defensiveness because I have used it when it benefits me. It has taken me years and a lot of self-reflection in order to address why and how I have been a white feminist, and, even so, I still fuck up. I don't want any white women to think that fucking up is the problem; it isn't. Not trying and not learning from our mistakes is the problem.

You yourself might fall under this white feminism category and not even realize it. If you have ever put your own emotions or needs above those of a minority woman, if you have ever asked women of color to explain to you how your behavior or language has been that of a white feminist without looking online or reading books on the subject matter for answers yourself, if you've used the friendship of a black or brown woman as a guardrail to protect yourself from the terrifying crash of being told you did something racist, if you've just dismissed wholesale a situation with a woman of color because the conversation made you too uncomfortable . . . you might be a white feminist, too. In my lifetime, I have been guilty of doing all of these things. I wholly own them. And I hope my ownership inspires other white women to do the same. If we want equality, then we must enact it equally.

White feminism is not reserved for white women alone. There are white men who also consider themselves to be feminist allies, but whose allegiance to gender still aligns with their preference for their own race. Look no further than the wage gap between black and white women across industries where men are often in control of who is being hired. According to data from the US Census Bureau in 2018, white women make roughly eighty cents on the dollar that every man does, but black women make half of that amount. White women are almost twice as likely to get hired by a white man over a black female peer with the same qualifications. Recently the Academy of Motion Picture Arts and Sciences accepted a record number of women into their membership, bringing the number of female members up to 31 percent from 28 percent overall. But women of color still make up less than half of that 31 percent.

White feminism is also not reserved for any specific age. Many white women who were part of the more intersectional second wave have had a hard time accepting the rejection of their work and all the complexities of the newest fourth wave's conversation. Both Gloria Steinem and Madeleine Albright famously caught heat for admonishing young women for not voting for Hillary Clinton in 2016. They were speaking from the experiences of their own wave, which has its purpose and its own hurdles to overcome. But since then, women have been able to have far more nuanced and intrapersonal conversations about where the fundamental problems lie— and the discussion cannot be one predominantly between two sexes of the same race anymore. It is a problem between the races and classes of different kinds of women, and even deeper, of a country that has outgrown the cisgender paradigm.

LASTLY, to my fellow white women reading this, take a moment now to ask yourself whether anything in this chapter has put your guard up and made you think to yourself, *Well, that's not true of me . . . or is it?* As author and activist Audre Lorde so powerfully put it, "What woman here is so enamored of her own oppression that she cannot see her heelprint upon another woman's face? What woman's terms of oppression have become precious and necessary to her as a ticket into the fold of the righteous, away from the cold winds of self-scrutiny?" Put your defenses down. Let go. Listen. And learn. We have a whole world to change and help grow, and it cannot be done without our participation and our greatest humility. This chapter would not be complete or reflective of its intention without putting its objective to action— without walking my own talk. So I've asked my friend Airea D. Matthews, prolific poet and assistant professor and director of creative writing at Bryn Mawr College, to join me in the conversation of this chapter. Here she illuminates our history and sheds light on the importance of the individual journey for all different kinds of women.

AMBER TAMBLYN

In Response to Sister Solidarity
by Airea D. Matthews

When issuing the call for women's solidarity in the
age of intersection, I find it necessary to consider
the central issues at stake for different groups of
women. Over the last twenty-five years, these more
fundamental issues have become harder to identify and easier to dismiss. As activists we've been
given a new model in Kimberlé Crenshaw's intersectional formulations from the early '90s, which
changed the way people perceived and performed
their identities. Instead of being constrained by a
crude taxonomy in which women were only black,
white, Hispanic, or Indigenous, crossroads of self-
classification have opened, including sexual ori-
entation, class, combinatory ethnicity, and modes
of oppression. While this may bolster the strength
of intersectional feminism, the original racial and
ethnic fractures have evolved into myriad fissures
that distinguish women across every imaginable
genotypical and phenotypical characteristic, and
thereby make the exigencies of specific feminisms
less clear.

Ironically, our epistemological advances around
identity structures have us asking the same question Toni Cade Bambara offered in 1970 in her preface to *The Black Woman*: "Are women after all simply

women?"* The question itself seeks to draw out reductive practices in feminism. In fact, one could argue that intersectionality is a practice of reductionism, because, in the case of black feminism, it liberally conflates blackness with all else, a certain watered-down multiculturalism. In James Bliss's article "Black Feminism Out of Place," he characterizes intersectionality as "a carceral logic," a way to capture and, perhaps, rehabilitate black thought. Bliss writes, ". . . this logic of capture or desire toward enclosure renders Black women as buried subjectivity."† With this in mind, I hope to respond to the concept of sisterly solidarity not as one woman taking on the voice of all women, or as a woman taking on an intersectional voice. I speak only as a black woman aware of her own intersections, who finds black feminist practice most representative of my history and experience.

At the time Bambara was writing her preface, the second wave of feminism, largely spearheaded by elite white women who had the time and status to be enraged, was entering its second decade of deliberations around sexual agency, workplace earnings,

---

* Toni Cade Bambara, ed., *The Black Woman: An Anthology* (New York: Washington Square, [1970] 2005).
† James Bliss, "Black Feminism Out of Place," *Signs: Journal of Women in Culture and Society,* 41, no. 4 (2016).

and de facto disparities. Meanwhile, black women continued to struggle under the same system with far worse results. In 1970, the year *The Black Woman* was published, black women earned 48.2 percent of white men's wages, while white women earned 58.7 percent.* From a labor perspective, we've known for decades that women and people of color were moved into, as if by an invisible hand, occupations with slow wage growth. This practice took a far greater toll on black women, who were usually wedged into the lowest paying jobs without the benefit of advancement, further widening wage gaps. The 2014 Census Bureau data bears this out as we see "white women earn 79 percent of white men, while black women earn 63 percent,"† which shows the wage gap between black women and white women effectively widened between 1970 and 2014. Said differently, the metric of white women's workplace inequality did not accurately measure the degree of economic and social distance that black women must confront. For black women the degrees of persistent alienation in the

---

* National Committee on Pay Equity, "The Wage Gap Over Time: In Real Dollars, Women See a Continuing Gap," Census Bureau reports and data, Current Population Reports, "Median Earning of Workers 15 Years Old and Over by Work Experience and Sex"; pay-equity.org/info-time.html.
† US Census Bureau, "Income and Earnings Summary Measures by Selected Characteristics: 2013 and 2014," in *Income and Poverty in the United States;* census.gov/programs -surveys/demo/tables/p60/252/table1.pdf.

workplace, home life, and in national participations make separate platforms and voices a necessity.

And, of course, black women recognize the importance of economic equity, and it is certainly not untrue that white male institutionality alienates all women. Yet there remain distinct contours to feminist realities deeply influenced by culture and history. The historical black American experience places its subjects at constant odds with the intertwined oppressions of race, color, class, sexism, and regionalism, all of which are mediated in a socially and economically unstable environment. Black feminism serves to address the hyper-specificities of what it means to be free from the perils of slavery but subject to white scrutiny and, oftentimes, tyranny in those environs. Our most recent news cycles bring to the fore recurrent instances of white scrutiny, often imposed by white women, such as: the incessant policing of the black body in public space (from BBQ Becky to Apartment Patty, and all in between), false accusations of sexual aggression (from pre–Emmett Till to a nine-year-old boy in a Brooklyn bodega), violent protections of property and, by extension, white women's virtue (from Trayvon Martin to the Dallas man killed in his own apartment by a white female officer). Black feminism asks for an end to the imaginative failures of a harmful white gaze, often enacted by the same white women who ask for our endorsements. But these recurring instances, which often turn lethal, make the need for freedom of movement and action of tantamount importance. In Angela Davis's "Lectures on Liberation," she directly addressed two specific freedoms: thought and action. Freedom of thought culminates in the outright rejection of oppression. Freedom of action demands the "liberty to move, to act in a way one chooses."* If feminism at its core, borrowing language from Foucault, is a "practice of freedom,"† then, possibly, where these feminisms diverge is in their exercise of those freedoms. It's implausible to fully understand these feminisms without interrogating why each seeks freedom, from whom they are seeking freedom, and to what end they are seeking freedom.

One of the primary cautions around white feminism is what Adrienne Rich coined "white solipsism," or the tendency "to think, imagine, and speak as if whiteness described the world."‡ Which is to say, the issues of white women have never served

---

* Angela Y. Davis, "Lectures on Liberation," in *Narrative of the Life of Frederick Douglass, an American Slave, Written by Himself: A New Critical Edition* (San Francisco: City Lights Open Media, 2010).

† Michel Foucault, "The Ethics of the Concern of the Self as a Practice of Freedom," in *Ethics*, Paul Rabinow, ed. (New York: New Press, 1997).

‡ Adrienne Rich, "Disloyal to Civilization: Feminism, Racism, Gynephobia," in *On Lies, Secrets, and Silence: Selected Prose 1966–1978* (New York: W. W. Norton & Company, 1979).

to reflect those of black women, or truly any other women outside of white women. American race, whether it is argued to be a social experiment or an economic imperative, carries different histories and positional relationships to white men. Because of white women's adjacency to power, much of the white feminist ethos, across generations, seems determined to establish their own power while protecting existing power structures. We see this enacted in the ways white feminists attempt to legitimize their platform; they petition existing power structures to center their concerns via legislation. The problem enters when they assume that their concerns are all inclusive. This is, in fact, at the root of what Amber Tamblyn calls "white defensiveness" (see page 174)— when white women are perplexed that their activism is not representative. Whether white women want to admit it or not, they benefit—directly and/or tangentially—from white supremacy, a system of exclusion. This protection frees their activism from being solely centered on their most basic needs— security, safety, sustenance, and shelter. At the present moment, the needs of the white feminist are largely psychological—a drive for belonging, being heard and believed, and an insistence on accomplishment. In this, white feminism concerns itself chiefly with visibility and status while ascribing secondary importance to legitimacy.

Conversely, black feminism finds its origins in

two waves. The first wave was led by black aboli-
tionists between 1830 and 1860, which shifted to issues of suffrage after the Civil War. The second wave
emerged in the civil rights era. The tie between the
two waves is the emancipatory struggle from the
power structures that sought to withhold physical
and psychological freedoms. This is to say, black
feminism's history is not based on distal access to
power but on its proximal relationship to slavery;
the latter drastically alters expectations from white
patriarchal structures. From the outset, the white
feminist was, at least, viewed as human not as chat-
tel. As a black feminist, I am not at all concerned with
protecting any established powers that actively resist ideals of humanism. Historically, those systems
do not exist to protect people like me, or others who
look like me. Unlike white feminists, I do not remind
white men of their mothers, wives, daughters, or sisters. I remind white men of a lost economy, of lost
opportunity, power slippages, and defeat. As such, I
find it difficult to believe that any system led by men
(or women) who benefit from oppression can be re-
habilitated. Why petition a beneficiary of oppression
to end a regime that enriches them? It's antitheti-
cal. If anything, black feminism hopes to dismantle
the prejudices and prohibitions that have been the
source of historical pain and trauma. Much of what
matters to the black feminist is based on survival—
the most basic requirements. We simply want to live

a life in which we establish self-definitions free from the violence, conflations, or reductions of the white gaze that causes great psychic and physical violence against black bodies. In this, as a black feminist, I do not privilege any status or legitimacy conferred by a system that has never, in ideology or practice, fully viewed me as equal or as a woman. Our primary goal is to exist without contestation. We are not seeking to be heroes; we seek to stay alive.

Despite these obvious observations, I find many white women who are still confounded by the black feminist hesitation to raise a collaborative banner. If anyone has paid any attention to what's happened to black Americans over the last two centuries, they would find some disturbing trends, including: large-scale erasure; fetishizing the black body while coopting the material culture; criminalizing race; disproportionate poverty; wealth and wage disparity; and premature death. They might also find a healthy contingent of activists who refuse to ignore how the patriarchy, and those adjacent to it, benefit from these trends. So, yes, we all grow weary of having to explain these patterns and their relationships, but we still find ourselves explaining these patterns and relationships. In simple terms of building trust, it would go a long way if white feminists would do some of that work for themselves. Listen and go forth. Reach people who are not apt to listen to a black woman. Find your cousins, your colleagues, your mothers, their mothers, your friends, and be a trusted guide for them. I am simply a lone voice proclaiming that white and black feminisms differ ideologically and offering reasons why. Nevertheless, one day, I'd love nothing more than to sit at a table of equals, celebrating a future that's returned after captivity. But that celebration will come when it's due. Right now, working together means wrestling with our differences in order to understand the ways in which we contribute to each other's oppression. Working together will never mean prioritizing the needs of white women and subsuming our own for the cause of oneness. Sisters, our emancipations will not be filtered through a dogma of "oneness," or subtle erasures but, rather, as a result of conscientiously accepting one another as being distinct and equal and free and human and here, for good.

16

When thinking about how to expand feminism's defining principles to make it a more inclusive ideology, it's most important to consider not only who has been left out of its representation, but also who has been left out of its shaping. In order for feminism to grow, its models must be wholly encompassing and reflective of the world, not just womankind. While feminism is about advocacy for women's rights, its larger goal is, and always has been, the equality of the sexes. As in, *all* identities and life experiences. I sat down with my friend Meredith Talusan, nonbinary trans author, journalist, and founding editor of the digital platform *them,* to talk feminism, inclusion, uprisings, what the past has taken, and what the future must bring, for all of us.

AMBER: When was the first time that you felt you identified as a feminist or even believed in it or cared about the idea of feminism?

MEREDITH: It was very shortly after I was introduced to feminism in college. I was an English major. One piece that I very, very clearly remember that we read was "Castration or Decapitation?" by French theorist Hélène Cixous. It basically revises the idea of the castration complex, of Freud's misogynist theory that men are afraid of being castrated and turned into women. Basically, what Cixous says is that if men are afraid of being castrated, women are afraid of being decapitated, because whenever women express their intelligence and their intellect in the face of patriarchy, they're immediately under threat. Women in Western patriarchal society are threatened in a very particular way by being valued primarily for their beauty, for qualities other than their brain. Reading that essay coincided with reading a lot of other things that informed me. Works from Virginia Woolf like *Mrs. Dalloway,* the Brontës. I remember reading this really amazing Christina Rossetti poem called "Sleeping at Last." And Sylvia Plath. Also, I was fifteen when I moved to the US from the Philippines. I had only been here in the States for a few years at the point when I was reading these works, so living under a patriarchy was foreign to me—it wasn't necessarily ingrained in me from a young age. This made it so that when I came here, I could really see it, clearly and abruptly. I didn't grow up in this culture—this culture of controlling women and the total authority of men. I grew up in the Philippines, where before colonial influence, indigenous Filipino society was extremely gender equitable. Both men and women could inherit land. It was understood that women could take over business affairs when husbands died. The way that people took on names is that if a woman is from a more prominent family, then the husband took the woman's name. This is just one of the examples of indigenous Filipino society and their attitude toward women having power. So the issue of women's inequality in the West was not familiar to me until I got to college here in the United States. And this was pre-transition, this was before I identified as trans. It was just, like, viscerally stunning, reading those texts and absorbing how unfair things were for women—the very idea that women are in some way inferior just really flew in the face of everything I believed in.

AMBER: That's a powerful and sobering way to be introduced to a culture, both by being thrown directly into it, but then also transitioning into the very gender you understood to be seen as inferior. It's like, "Guess what? The world hates women! Also, by the way, you're a woman."

MEREDITH: I know, right? I actually ended up writing my undergraduate thesis on this play called *The Tragedy of Mariam,* which is the first play written by a woman, published in England in 1613, and is about the abusive marriage between Herod and his biblical second wife, Mariam, which actually ends with Herod ordering Mariam's decapitation because she wants a divorce from him.

AMBER: Decapitation!

MEREDITH: Off with their heads! Also, the woman who wrote that play, Elizabeth Cary, had to publish it anonymously, because she would be dishonored as a woman writing such plays in 1613. Also, her husband put her under house arrest, essentially, because she wanted to convert to Catholicism.

AMBER: Oh, yes. Women are property.

MEREDITH: Yes, women's bodies are property but also, women's creativity is also somehow the property of men as well.

AMBER: The idea of women having to live under anonymity in order to be taken seriously, in order to call out sexual harassment or assault, and in order just to survive, it's breathtaking, the kinds of masks we have to wear in order to thrive.

MEREDITH: Exactly. So certainly by senior year of college and reading those stories and works, I was definitely calling myself a feminist.

AMBER: Did that definition change for you once you transitioned? Did you feel more weight with it, or did you feel more separated by it? Did you feel anything different, or did you feel even closer to it after?

MEREDITH: I was just so focused on the transition and all of the crises around transitioning that I wasn't really paying attention to the ways in which I was actually absorbing all of these problematic gender norms. For most of the world, belonging actually means absorbing all of these patriarchal systems and tropes. And I would actually say that the pressure on trans women is even greater in a lot of ways than cis women.

AMBER: Absolutely. I agree.

MEREDITH: Because as a cis woman you can be called unwomanly if you don't behave like a "typical woman," but if you're a trans woman and you don't behave like a typical woman, you're a man. Your entire identity is under attack.

AMBER: It's far more threatening.

MEREDITH: Yeah. When I was in grad school, I did an MFA in fiction at Cornell. There was this guy in my class who was doing this craft talk that had these graphs in it, and the graphs were inaccurate. I knew this to be true because right after undergrad I was a technical assistant at MIT, and part of my job was to design figures for scientific papers. So I raised my hand, and I had learned through socialization that I needed to soft-pedal if I'm questioning a man's judgment, so I framed my query as a question. It was just like, "Oh, can you clarify this? I'm not sure about . . . There seems to be an inaccuracy here," or whatever. Then he repeated his same explanation with the wrong graph. Then I said, "I still don't understand." Then he said, "This is basic math, Meredith." That's something that I will never forget.

AMBER: Wow.

MEREDITH: The other thing was that as soon as he said that, the thing that popped in my head was, *Oh my God, did you make a mistake, Meredith?* That was the moment when I realized that I would have never thought that pre-transition. Pre-transition, I would've told him flat out that he was wrong, that I was a technical assistant at MIT for several years, that I had taken advanced math classes. This guy is a person who's in an MFA program in literature who has no scientific background. Why would I think that his judgment is in some way superior to mine? I think that was the moment when I told myself: You really need to monitor this misogynistic shit, because you're absorbing it without even knowing it.

AMBER: That is fascinating and so incredibly powerful. I don't think I had even considered the double oppression of that paradox. Of the idea that transitioning is supposed to be freeing, but for trans women, it actually sometimes isn't because you are forced by society to absorb our gendered bullshit.

MEREDITH: Exactly. And here's the other truth. There's something important about the ways in which the trans woman's experience is intuitively feminist, because I will always have a comparative perspective. I always have this super-strong sense that, no, a man wouldn't have treated me a certain way pre-transition. He wouldn't have interrupted me at this meeting. He wouldn't have questioned my judgment. This is not a guess—this is my literal comparative experience. I literally know the difference in treatment.

AMBER: This is so true and something I hope the cis men who read this book will really absorb and think about—all two of my cis male readers. Hey, guys!

MEREDITH: Ha! Hey, woke dudes reading this!

AMBER: Thank you for taking time away from playing Destiny on Xbox to read this interview. Or is it Playstation? Anyway, Meredith and I thank you.

MEREDITH: They should be thanking us, actually.

AMBER: Oh, they will be. They will be.

MEREDITH: You know, as somebody who now manages people, as an editor of *them,* I point this out all the time to female coworkers and people to whom I am a boss. I was managing a team at work, and there was this pattern that emerged where a male employee kept asserting himself and essentially performing the task of a female employee peer. I said to her, "Do you notice how he's behaving, like he's the one who's supposed to be generating the ideas when you're supposed to be the one who is giving him tasks? That's not right." What kind of effect does this have on bosses like me when it comes time to promote someone? When you see these types of gender disparities as completely normal? I believe it's easier for me to identify than had I been born cis.

AMBER: I feel like this is also applicable between white women and women of color. Watch a room where only women are present and you will see the white women present themselves like cis men, talking over women of color and generally dominating the topics and narratives. And white women do that because they too have been so desperate to be the arbiters of their dialogues, their own futures and destinies. We are so hungry to be seen that we go blind in the process. What do you think of the term "white feminism"? I imagine you have a very different relationship with that term, considering you are not only trans but also albino. How does that term affect you or sit with you?

MEREDITH: It's funny because I think, in part, because I grew up in a different country and I am Filipino, I'm very, very internally a person of color. My politics are super, super aligned with POC politics, but I move through the world most of the time being perceived as white. As a result, I deeply understand the term and I've seen white feminism from both sides: I've seen it in action in white women, and I've seen it in action in myself. For instance, I had this experience recently where I was late for my flight. I was at the airport. My flight was leaving in fifteen minutes, and I was just in near tears because I was going to miss this flight trying to get through security. It was the only flight that day. I was giving a keynote. This white woman saw me in the security line, motioned me over, and allowed me to cut in front of her. It was only when I was safely out of security that

I thought to myself, *Why? Would she have done it had I been visibly brown and trans?* Even if she did, the other thing that I noticed about myself is that I asked myself whether this tearful reaction is in some way socially conditioned, because I do tend . . . I have found that it does affect people when I cry, in a way that's different from when women of color cry. Those dynamics are happening for me at a micro level, but I think that if you expand that to a macro level, there are a number of issues involved. That if one demographic of women gets more sympathy than other kinds of women, that's definitely a big problem and indicative of the larger way in which we value women who are not cis and/or white. Have you heard of Carole Pateman?

AMBER: Yes.

MEREDITH: She wrote *The Sexual Contract,* which looks at the way women in Western societies have been foundationally beholden to men—that there's sort of this deal that was struck: Women can exist and lead relatively fruitful, happy lives as long as they're subservient to men.

AMBER: Right, both at home and in the workplace.

MEREDITH: Both at home and in the workplace, but the thing is that that original structure happened at a time when black people were enslaved, where forced labor was being used in colonies, when obviously any notion of gender nonconformity or alternative sexuality was shut down. There's a very real entire legacy of white women being able to derive protection from the patriarchy as long as they accept that they're subservient to men.

AMBER: Two words: Susan. Collins. What she did to women by voting for Judge Kavanaugh is unforgivable.

MEREDITH: Yeah, she's like the sacrificial lamb the Republican men used.

AMBER: There is a perfect example of someone who benefited from her place within a white patriarchal system and felt no problem carrying on that tradition—of just keeping her place in the long line of white women who feel fortunate to be in a position of power and so won't do anything to jeopardize that position for the greater good, because, frankly, they don't have to.

MEREDITH: Yes, so true. There are a number of things that I think minorities find frustrating about white feminism. One is what you just touched on, this idea that white feminists are often not used to being confronted about the ways in which they oppress other people, and when they do—

AMBER: They cry.

MEREDITH: Yes, they cry.

AMBER: White as a hotel towel tears.

MEREDITH: Ha! I've done it too, actually, to be perfectly fair. It's hard. It's hard not to. But we can't use our own oppression as a justification for oppressing other people.

AMBER: Yep.

MEREDITH: This also goes for the trans community. Some people can't possibly fathom being called transphobic when they themselves have experienced real misogyny. Because what's actually the case is that being oppressed should ideally make you more sensitive to the oppression of others.

AMBER: One could apply that not just to individuals but to communities of people as well. For instance, what's been happening between Israel and Palestine for generations. One would imagine that a community that suffered from such brutal human rights atrocities would not turn a blind eye to atrocities of a similar nature happening right under their noses.

MEREDITH: Yes, it's a really common phenomenon. For instance, sometimes gay white men can be extremely transphobic toward trans women and you think to yourself, *Really? After all the homophobia you've had to put up with in your life?*

AMBER: What about feminist author Chimamanda Ngozi Adichie and her comments that trans women will never be able to truly understand the female experience?

MEREDITH: There is so much of that.

AMBER: I'm such a fan of her work and this was such a disheartening thing to hear her say. It's such an empathic disconnect for someone so deeply in tune. I understand where she's coming from, in wanting to protect a woman's experience and story, but this is not at all the right way to do it. Feminism must have an allegiance not to a gender but to an ideal. To the belief that anyone can be valued as a woman, should they identify as that. Othering the trans community from the real harm and pain you have experienced trying to merely live in this world seems quite hypocritical to me.

MEREDITH: Right. It's really fascinating to me when cis women are asked for their opinion about trans women—Chimamanda being one of them. At some level, there's also a degree to which I wonder: Why is she put in a position of having expertise around the relationship between trans women's experiences and cis women's experiences? Her comments were really, really disappointing. I feel like somebody needs to have a nuanced conversation with her about it, and nobody really has as far as I know.

AMBER: You would be great at that.

MEREDITH: I'd love to. Because I adore her, too. I think she's done really important work. And circling back to your question around transition and feminism, I was significantly more accepted as a male feminist than I am as a trans feminist. That should tell you a lot about how trans women are valued. People were very complimentary about my feminist values before I transitioned. Now any article that I write that in some way tries to confront or talk about the condition of women, I get multiple comments.

AMBER: What do the comments say?

MEREDITH: Oh, things like, "What do you know about being a woman? You're a man." Your motivations are questioned. And all of this leads me to believe that when we say that men are the problem, the reality is that gender is the problem, right? Gender is the problem, and it manifests in us, in this society, creating a world where a particular set of people get all of these benefits that another set of people don't simply because they have one set of genitalia. Once you consider that from a different perspective, then you see how it doesn't make sense to say something like, "Why is this man trying to speak for us? Why is this man trying to act like we don't know or that we can't fight for ourselves?" The truth is feminism must be—not just *should* be—wholly inclusive. We want as many people as possible to be feminists! That's good for womankind! You know what I mean?

AMBER: Absolutely.

MEREDITH: Over the years, I have experienced some major issues with transphobic cis women, especially in early transition.

AMBER: Do you feel comfortable sharing any of those stories?

MEREDITH: Actually, the most recent example was, I was in grad school and I was living in a graduate student co-op. A student who was a woman found out I was trans and said, "Oh, so you're actually really a man." And when I asked her to clarify, she said, "So you're a man who cut his dick off to be a woman."

AMBER: Jesus Christ.

MEREDITH: Literally, in public at the dinner table, these types of comments.

AMBER: How recently was this?

MEREDITH: 2012.

AMBER: This is terrible, Meredith.

MEREDITH: It's a very common form of aggression used against the trans community. These types of comments are actually very similar to people who've been sexually harassed, cis or otherwise. At first, you try to make light of it. You try to excuse it, and you don't really pay attention to how it's affecting you until you can't anymore.

AMBER: Good comparison.

MEREDITH: What's really interesting and upsetting about that situation was that that woman was able to utilize the instinctive drive of people to protect women for her own benefit. I feel like if my transphobic harasser had been a man, it would've been a clearer form of understood transphobia and people would be okay with me calling it that. Again, the gender problem comes into play. But somehow the idea of a woman being oppressive to another woman is something that is very difficult for people to see as real. As a result, in situations where cis women are oppressive toward trans women, that often goes either ignored, denied, or unacknowledged, because their transphobia is couched and disguised in the notion that they are fighting for a kind of woman's rights that somehow trans women are not a part of.

AMBER: I have often said this: Who hates women more than Donald Trump does? Other women.

MEREDITH: Yep.

AMBER: That's because there is a scarcity mentality.

MEREDITH: Right. Absolutely.

AMBER: This sense of, "I barely exist, and so I'm not comfortable with there being a larger definition of the way in which I can barely exist, because that makes room for my existence even smaller, my fight even harder, my success less possible." That message is so sad to me: That not only can we not contain multitudes as individual women, but in the very identity of womanhood itself. This kind of poisoned thinking was not created by cis women—it was created by a patriarchal doctrine—but it is absolutely perpetuated by cis women, and that is a huge problem: The controlling of our collective definition—who women are allowed to be, but also, who women are NOT allowed to be.

MEREDITH: Yes, exactly.

AMBER: I have asked myself this question: Who gets to control the definition? The definition of feminism? I always get asked in interviews, "What is your definition of feminism?" It always makes me laugh, because everyone is searching for the perfect definition of what it is, and I think the greatest problem with feminism is the obsession with its perfect definition, with the purity, perfection, and precision of the definition. In the same way that women are upheld to a purity mentality—if you are not the most qualified, the most attractive, physically abled, if you are not the perfect definition—then you do not get to count. I think the need to define feminism is the larger problem, which is why Roxane Gay's *Bad Feminist* was so revolutionary as a concept. This idea that there is not one form of feminism that is correct or right and that it's okay to not adhere to the rules of what former waves of feminism or people have believed is correct about it. Its very ideals and nature are mercurial and must move and shift as our culture does. It must move and shift for the sake of its future, not for the sake of preserving its past.

MEREDITH: I think part of what is frustrating for minorities who are not women is that part of the reason that men have engaged in bad social conditioning is that it serves those types of women. Also, women are the only marginalized group that actually has the numbers to fully threaten men. That woman who confronted Jeff Flake during the Kavanaugh hearings, that is the type of civil disobedience that we need right now, and I feel like, speaking of frustrations with white feminism, there aren't enough white feminists who are willing to be confrontational in that way. It's like white female social conditioning is getting in the way of us being able to really create the change we need. The Women's March was fine and all, but where's the disobedience? Where's the real fight? Trans women have a long history in America of civil disobedience. Trans women were able to change laws in San Francisco, Compton's cafeteria riot, and, obviously, trans women were able to advance queer rights through the Stonewall riots. Those are legacies that trans women embody, especially trans women of color. One of the things that I observed is, a lot of times minority representatives of movements get asked to adhere to the established norms of the majority, right? We're made to do that when it should be the other way around, because black and trans women have a lot of experience confronting this type of oppression in extremely impactful ways. For instance, look at Black Lives Matter and the powerful impact it has had on our society—and that organization is only a few years old! It concerns me, because I feel like there are generations of distrust between different kinds of women, the least of which is generations of white women colluding with white men to keep black people enslaved.

AMBER: That's absolutely correct, yeah.

MEREDITH: It's just very hard to unify as a feminist movement around that, right?

AMBER: Yes.

MEREDITH: I worked on a trans murder case in the Philippines for several years. It was a murder of a trans woman by a US Marine, and from the very beginning there was no question. There are no substantial politics around excluding trans women in the definition of women in the Philippines, in part, because there's no history of one group—

AMBER: Of two genders. There's not the two-gender system.

MEREDITH: There's not the two-gender system, yes, but also, there's more gender parity overall. And we don't have the racism factor in our history like it exists in the US—a legacy in which one demographic of women has subjugated another demographic of women.

AMBER: Our misogyny transcends gender *and* race.

MEREDITH: Exactly. One of the things that I really notice as a major difference between Filipino and American society is that Americans are very, very obsessed with identifying the differences between each other, whereas Filipinos are always trying to create a connection with you and figure out how you're similar and the same to them. If I introduce myself to a Filipino stranger, the first thing they'll say is, "What is your last name?" And after learning the last name, they will try to figure out if they know anybody else with that last name, and then, "Oh, where are you from in the Philippines?" They would just be like, "Oh, I have a coworker who comes from your province, and do you know them?" There is just a deep sense of togetherness there. Of not dividing.

AMBER: How can we change these practices and definitions for womanhood and feminism? What are good steps for people who might be totally clueless?

For instance, what about someone who doesn't have a Meredith Talusan in their lives, who maybe lives in a place where they don't have access to these types of conversations and friendships? I know for me as a white woman, it's imperative that I have difficult conversations with other white women. That I spend as much time protesting a Susan Collins as I do picking up the phone and talking to my Republican white aunt whose ear I actually have. White women have to do more of this work and stop pretending like it's not a major part of misogyny's pervasiveness, because it is.

MEREDITH: Yes, I agree. And I think that that might be the most important thing. Find a way to connect with people who are not like you—even white liberal women talking to conservative white women. Specifically, as a feminist, as a white feminist, find a way to put your privilege aside. It's going to be hard, because one of the things that white feminists do, or white women in general do with minorities, is they try to cultivate friendships with minorities, but it's very hard for them to let go of that privilege, so they can be really blind to it in some ways. And I think white women really do have to step up to the plate and do the hard work of talking to other white women. It's in this communication and understanding that we will find greater, better change for all of womankind.

17

A mere ten days after Jodi Kantor and her coauthor Megan Twohey broke the story of Harvey Weinstein's extensive history of sexual harassment and assault, Woody Allen quite predictably became the first man to publicly vocalize the worst fear lingering in the back of most men's minds. In a BBC News interview, Allen said that he felt for the "poor women" who were assaulted, but was worried about a "witch hunt atmosphere" taking hold of the country. He quickly tried to clean up that mess of a comment by condemning Weinstein's actions, but the subtext of his fear had already been unloaded on like minds.

The witch hunt atmosphere—as well as being a great name for an all-girl punk band—was something a lot of men were quietly whispering to each other about, some even directly to me. Quentin Tarantino told me that he had run into a popular male movie star on a plane recently, a man who is a self-proclaimed feminist, who had expressed that the fallout from the #MeToo movement very well may be that men just won't want to hire women anymore. There were fearful rumblings of potential false allegations and revengeful ex-lady-lovers and "crazy" women raising hell in the lives of oh-so-virtuous men. Talk of an atmosphere of witch-hunting sounded more like a narrative belonging to a paranoid supremacy rather than the long history of twisting women's intentions against them.

A male playwright texted me to ask about the future of "innocent until proven guilty," a concept that this #MeToo movement seemed to be destroying with "reckless abandon." I have often contemplated the phrase "innocent until proven guilty" and the presumption of innocence as a first rule when applied outside of a courtroom. To make a presumption is to make a choice to side with one party over another without consideration. This raises the question: What's the point of weighing anything when the scale is already imbalanced? While I understand and respect the importance of this principle within the judicial system, I question its misappropriation outside of the law. It strikes me as an exploitation exacted by problematic men who hide behind it willy-nilly as though it can be applied anywhere, at any time, under the auspices of their entitlement. Outside of a courtroom—and sometimes even in it—"innocent until proven guilty" can't help but be flawed, much like many of the laws created by our forefathers, whose intentions have naturally eroded over time (such as the right to bear arms in a world of printable 3-D guns).

"Presumed innocent until proven guilty" was coined by the English lawyer Sir William Garrow (1760–1840) in 1791. His aim was to force accusers to thoroughly present evidence in a court of law to back up their claims. Sir William was a defense lawyer during the wild era of swift trials in England—trials that often lasted ten minutes and seemed more like reality shows for blood-hungry audiences than what we know of prosecutions today. Countersuits didn't even exist until the late 1800s and SLAPP laws (strategic lawsuits against public participation), which are intended to intimidate and silence a case's critics, were not introduced until 1980.

Garrow was not thinking about a judicial world in which plaintiffs are burdened with frivolous discovery requests, tying lawyers up with meaningless hours of paperwork, purposefully racking up legal fees, and wasting their time. He was not thinking about the world of social media. He was not thinking about these types of aggressions because he didn't have to: they simply didn't exist in Victorian England, or nineteenth-century America for that matter. He was not thinking about how the idea would be applied peripherally or futuristically in themes of consequence outside of his own judicial vernacular. And so here we are in 2019, stuck with the language of a defining principle that is so valuable and yet so vandalized.

I'm not suggesting doing away with the burden of proof—that would be insane. I understand that this principle protects many people in a court of law and is not always used vindictively. Sir William himself used the presumption of innocence to rightfully defend teenage chambermaids who were raped and impregnated by their masters, only to be charged with infanticide when they gave birth on their own and the newborns died. If those cases were tried in contemporary courts, it would be the masters using the presumption of innocence to defend themselves against statutory rape charges (though only one in five sexual assault cases ever goes to trial). I do question, though, what can be done to stop the egregious use of this principle by people who do not fully understand it. The hypocrites who denounce courts of public opinion are the same ones who use the language of the legal system to defend themselves within courts of public opinion but *only* when doing so benefits them.

What would William Garrow think of today's world, where accusations can be made with the push of a button and cases can be wrapped up for decades, instead of minutes, in bureaucratic loopholes, technicalities, and manipulation tactics? A world where his principle is used by anyone, for any reason, in any context? "Innocent until proven guilty" is often used as a weapon of mass destruction for aggressors who haphazardly award themselves immunity, from boardrooms to bedrooms and beyond. Their microaggressions have become macro-oppressions, unilaterally silencing and sidelining whole cultures, industries, and bodies of people.

Furthermore, how could today's microaggressions even be provable under Garrow's two-hundred-plus-year-old definition? How does someone prove that she was not hired because she is a woman or because she is black or because she is trans? How can you prove you were physically assaulted at work if you are a sex worker? How can you prove your boss put his hand on your thigh during a work dinner? Or that your voice and perspective have been repeatedly boxed out of important conversations in which they belong?

It has long been the burden of women and minorities to point out these grievances and find solutions for problems we did not create. We bear the burden of having to prove this not just in courts of law, but in the interrogation and dismantling of the very language that has never taken us into consideration. My hope is that in this ignited era, men will follow suit and begin to find it within themselves to do dogmatic diligence both by holding themselves accountable and perhaps, even more important, by holding one another accountable for dismantling the status quo. It is the only way to enlighten what has been in the dark for so long.

Not all men are witch hunt hyperbolists. I find myself talking to lots of men who want to be a part of the solution but don't know how to engage. And they don't know how to engage because they were never taught to in the first place. I can't place full blame on them for that. Blaming them for what was handed down to them through the history of masculinity would be like blaming myself for what has been handed down to me oppressively. But if ignorance can be a learned behavior, then so too can illumination, and it is within each of us to teach someone willing to grow, and to put our defenses down and receive the same gift in return. Which is why, while I do not place full blame on some well-meaning men's inability to engage, I do ask them for accountability and an open mind to learn, just as I ask this of myself. As Ashley Judd said to me over dinner one evening: "Once you become aware, you become responsible." And it's unacceptable to evade that responsibility just because it's tiring or uncomfortable or because society has made it so you don't have to.

ALMOST A YEAR AFTER Woody Allen's whispers of witch-hunting, he returned to the public eye to speak up again, but this time through his wife, Soon-Yi Previn, the adopted daughter of Allen's former partner Mia Farrow. Their romance began when Soon-Yi was twenty years old and Allen was in his fifties. I'm married to a man who is nineteen years my senior, so it's not the age gap itself that feels uncomfortably inappropriate, it is the lack of life experience tied with the fact that she was more or less his stepdaughter. (Allen was also accused of molesting Mia Farrow's youngest daughter, Dylan Farrow, when she was very young, an allegation that he has always denied.) Soon-Yi did an interview in *New York* magazine to talk about how unfairly she and her husband have been treated, and how misunderstood their relationship has been by the public. They complained about how they have become pariahs in the eyes of the nation, even having their campaign contribution returned by Hillary Clinton during her 2016 bid for president.

Respectfully, what I don't think Soon-Yi sees—or is capable of seeing from the inside of abuse, where there are often no windows from which to see out—is how her story fits perfectly into the behavioral patterns of her husband, whose entire body of artistic work has centered around themes of fetishizing female youth; of old men seducing, or being seduced by, impressionable yet not-so-innocent young women. And I do mean *young* women, as in the case with his film *Manhattan,* where Mariel Hemingway

plays Tracy, the seventeen-year-old girl his character, forty-two-year-old Isaac, is dating.

In the article, Soon-Yi talks a lot about the abuse
she endured at the hands of Mia Farrow while growing up in her house, a claim that other family members dispute. While this is terrible and nothing that
any child should ever have to suffer through if it is
true, it is still a distraction tactic that shifts the focus
away from the central problem at hand, and the reason anyone cares at all about this story in the first
place: that men like Woody Allen use their power to
groom young girls into partners they can influence
and ultimately control.

I'm sure Soon-Yi would take great offense in
hearing someone suggest that her more than twenty-
year marriage to Allen was somehow groomed by
him, but honestly, and with the utmost respect, I ask
this question: How could she know if it wasn't? I feel
comfortable asking this question because I was once
in a five-year relationship with a much older man as
well—the same ex-boyfriend I mentioned earlier in
this book. I lived with him and admired him for his
genius. It is not hard for me to see now, through a lot
of therapy and reflection, how truly groomed I was
by him because of my attraction to him, but also my
attraction to the power he held. I looked up to him,
valued his opinions on the world, and even excused
his violent outbursts and mood swings. I told myself
I was uniquely qualified to understand his tempera-

ment, and I wore the honor of that role in our relationship like a crown.

My parents were beside themselves with fear and
anger over my choice of a partner, but there was little
they could do, legally. I may have been a young adult,
nonetheless, I was still an adult. I was an extraordi-
narily willful young woman who used every ounce of
my magic to get what I wanted. I was that young girl
who had financial freedom because she had a full-
time job, which gave me the appearance of being able
to make adult decisions far before I should have. I
was that girl, ahead of her years, extremely curious
and hungry for the more dangerous experiences in
life. I was the girl who crashed her parents' car when
she was twelve years old because I was trying to hide
it from a neighbor I didn't like who they'd offered to
lend it to. I was that girl who talked an older friend
into taking me to get my nipples pierced when I was
sixteen. I was that girl who was suspended in high
school for fighting, who shoplifted from department
stores, who wanted to test the world and, in return,
be tested twice as hard.

I understand where Soon-Yi comes from when
she says, "I'm not a retarded little underage flower
who was raped, molested, and spoiled by some evil
stepfather—not by a long shot." I didn't want to hear
that I had no agency over my actions either, no matter how young I was. I didn't want to hear it from my
parents or my friends or anyone. In fact, the more

they pleaded—the more my father tried everything he could next to calling the police to get me to leave this man—the harder I leaned into the relationship. As I grew into my twenties with him, my views of the world continued to be informed by his. If he didn't like a friend of mine, that friend was gone. If I had done something to upset him, I would fix it by using my savings to buy him expensive presents. I was so deeply under the spell of his grooming that I could not even find it within me to leave him once he became abusive.

One day, I found a VHS tape in his backpack that he had secretly recorded of him having sex with another woman. Sitting on the living room floor of the apartment I shared with him, I forced myself to watch it. I was just about twenty years old, the same age as Soon-Yi was when she got together with Woody Allen. I later found out my boyfriend had been having an affair with the woman on the tape for the entire time we had been together. This was the man I had lost my virginity to, who I had fallen so deeply in love with, who I thought I understood more than anyone. When I confronted him about it outside of a club in Los Angeles, he spit in my face in front of many of our mutual friends. One of those friends, Danny Johnson, stepped between us to tell him what he had done was wrong, and he punched Danny in the face. By the end of the fight, they were both covered in blood from head to toe.

I share these painful memories to point out that none of this stopped me from staying with him. When I was sure he had slipped something into my coffee and then tried to coerce me into having sex while I could barely move, it didn't stop me from staying. The time he choked me over our couch while his friend sat watching didn't stop me from staying. The time he watched my father fall down a flight of stairs at the wrap party of the first season of *Joan of Arcadia* without doing a thing to help him because he was angry at me didn't stop me from staying. Whispering in my ear on the way to the CBS Upfronts that he was going to kill me soon did not stop me from staying. I was so deeply under his spell that I stayed with him for years. I stayed with him until his mental illness became so apparent, it was clear he actually might kill me—until I was forcibly removed from the relationship by the combined efforts of myself, my family, and my friends.

I do not tell you this story to compare Soon-Yi's cushy, Upper East Side, twenty-year marriage to that of my five-year volatile and abusive relationship. I tell you this story to remind people of the lengths young women who are groomed from a young age will go to in order to stay with their groomers in order to not break the spell. If I could stay with this man through all that, wouldn't it be possible for any woman, like Soon-Yi, to stay in an inappropriate relationship and grow out of the wrongness of her conditioning through the sheer passage of time? If her relationship with Woody Allen ended at some point, I wonder if Soon-Yi would be able to see the foundation of the relationship as being the source of the problem from the beginning. Maybe she wouldn't, who knows? But as one woman who was forced to examine her own grooming, I would say it's worth a try. Growth and discovery are worth a lifetime of trying.

While men are predominantly the ones who groom women from young ages, they are not the only ones who are guilty of this behavior. In the summer of 2018, I published the book that I had been writing throughout the 2016 election cycle, a novel called *Any Man,* which follows several men whose lives are haunted after they are sexually assaulted by a female serial rapist. I went on a very long thirty-four-city book tour, and by the end of it I had accrued a large stash of handwritten letters from those who had read the book and those who were about to. What was so startling was that every single one of them was written by men.

The content of the letters ranged in topic from the typical older autograph collector telling me that my book sounded "titillating" but that he hoped I'd "stick to acting instead," to a younger, quiet man who begged me to accept Jesus Christ as my Lord and Savior and that there was still time to stop "the sins of your words." As a former child actress who had more restraining orders against crazed male fans before the age of eighteen than I did hair scrunchies, I am no stranger to the creepy entitlement and ownership that some men feel they have over me. But this time, only a few of the letters referenced my acting career, and the rest revealed a startling yet important narrative: men are also sexually assaulted, and not only by other men but by women, too.

Men are not the only practitioners of sexual assault through coercion and grooming. The actress and activist Asia Argento was accused of sexually assaulting a seventeen-year-old named Jimmy Bennett, a boy who had played her son once in a film and had remained close to Argento as he got older. The news made me think of a fictional character in my novel named Ezra Fisher who is coerced into having sex at the age of ten by the antagonist, a woman who goes by the name of Maude. Much like what is needed in our culture today, the narrative in *Any Man* does not set out to reverse the gender roles of sexual assault stories, but instead to de-gender and thereby broaden the conversations surrounding sexual assault altogether. Because in order to have systemic, widespread change when it comes to rape and its illusive culture, we must have more inclusive and sometimes difficult conversations regarding who, exactly, is being assaulted. We must hold space not only for the majority of those who report assault but for the minority, too. Painting a whole picture of the problem is the only way we are going to put a spotlight on a whole solution. As Tarana Burke so perfectly and simply stated: "This movement is for all of us and there is no model survivor."

While women make up the majority of survivors by a wide margin (the highest number being American Indian women), one in ten men also reports being assaulted in his lifetime. And while that is not a large number, it must not be ignored. According to the National Center for Transgender Equality, 47 percent of the trans community report being sexually assaulted in their lifetime, and statistics in nonbinary communities are still being collected. But these are just statistics for those who actually report their assaults. What about those who don't? Where do they fit into this broadened conversation as a whole? According to the Rape, Abuse & Incest National Network (RAINN), the nation's largest anti–sexual violence organization, only two out of three sexual assaults are reported annually, which leaves more questions than it does answers. Without an understanding of the different kinds of bodies afflicted by sexual violence, we cannot do the full work to change the system that allows it to happen.

Part of the inclusivity we must start practicing is not just in identifying but in examining. One of the most upsetting details regarding Ms. Argento's story is that she paid off her accuser mere weeks after accusing Harvey Weinstein of doing the same thing to her. I am constantly reminded of how deeply rooted the cycle of abuse is, often turning the abused into abusers. Trauma breeds trauma unless it can be treated, which is a privilege saved for those who can afford treatment. And what happens to those who cannot? The truth is that a startling percentage of people who sexually assault have themselves been assaulted. The reciprocity of human cruelty gets handed down between battered psyches and bodies, becoming a snowball of emotional labor. The notion that hurt people hurt people is not just a saying, it is a statistical truth.

What would a world look like where hurt people helped people instead? Not by taking on the responsibility of healing others, but by simply affording them a space to be heard and believed? Is this not what was so powerful and important about the impact of millions of women coming forward recently with stories of sexual assault? By lifting up the most marginalized voices of those who are often left behind—by examining the whole of our physical burden, not just the largest part of it—we will be able not only to break the cycle of abuse but to banish it forever.

18

How the history books will describe Woody Allen's legacy is hard to say, and it's made me think about other men adjacent to him who have been swept up in the embers of this ignited era—the men in comedy. Last year, Louis C.K. made a surprise visit to the Comedy Cellar in New York City after his career was torpedoed by the news that he had masturbated in front of several women during meetings. Coincidentally (or maybe not), C.K. is an admirer of Woody Allen, and shortly before the news broke of his indiscretions, he was set to release a movie that he had written and directed with an eerily Woody Allen–like theme of older men grooming and preying on underage girls. My husband, who, full disclosure, has known Louis for more than twenty years, went to an early screening when Louis was looking for feedback on a cut of the film before it was finished. When he returned from the screening he said to me, "That movie is . . . It's going to get him in so much trouble, for so many reasons." Indeed, coupled with the stories of his sexual transgressions, the film never saw the light of day and proved to be another glaring example of just how tone-deaf some artists can be.

To my mind, C.K. wrote perhaps the most believable and acceptable apology letter out of any of the men who were called out during 2017's #MeToo movement. He ended it by saying, "I have spent my long and lucky career talking and saying anything I want. I will now step back and take a long time to listen." It is clear that Louis delivered on the first two promises in that sentence: to step back and to take a long time (sort of). But did he listen? The answer is most definitely: No, he didn't. In his return to the stage at the Comedy Cellar—an unannounced performance given without audience consent—he made absolutely no mention of his misdeeds and provided no reflection as to what exactly he had listened to and perhaps learned during his year of stepping back. Instead, he dog whistled with a rape whistle joke, as if signaling that he owed nothing to anyone—no explanation, no comment, no recourse—and neither did other men like him.

Louis C.K. is not the only comedian who has been

accused of doing something abusive only to steam-roll over the topic and carry on his merry way. In one of the more controversial stories to come out of the #MeToo reckoning, comedian Aziz Ansari was accused of heavily coercing a woman into coming back to his apartment to have sex when she didn't want to. Ansari laid low for a few months, only to reemerge later, untouched and ready for another international comedy tour. The American public was so hungry for its #MeToo backlash, so ready for Woody Allen's words to come true, that they pointed to this story about Aziz as nothing more than a bad date and an inevitable example of all the false allegations to come against men.

Similarly, a friend confided in me at a dinner party one night that she had been coerced and sexually assaulted by the creator of a popular TV show. He had lured her back to his house and gotten her drunk, wearing her down with requests to have sex until she finally "gave up and got it over with." Sound familiar? Upon seeing how the woman in the Ansari story was treated publicly, she said, "I don't want to say anything about it now. I'm too scared that I will end up like that woman."

There are two very large problems here that must be addressed during this intense time of radical examination and shifting the discourse about how we define and identify abuses of power. The first problem is in our understanding of what actually falls under the definitions and categories of an abuse of power, sexual or otherwise. Many men, and some women too, have been taught that sexual assault is defined by only the most simple of definitions. We define it like we see it in the movies: a man holds a woman down and covers her mouth and forces her to have sex with him. This is just one of many examples of sexual assault, and yet to most men's minds, it is the only example. Which is why when stories of Harvey Weinstein's unwanted cunnilingus of women came out, some people were genuinely confused about how this could qualify as sexual assault. Wouldn't that have to be consensual in order for him to even get down there and be able to do that? This is just one nonsensical example of the wrongheaded thinking about sexual assault that we have lived with. Some men don't believe that putting their fingers inside a woman while she's passed out is sexual assault, or even just forcing a kiss on someone, or putting a hand on someone's butt. Anytime anyone is physically touched in a sexual or flirtatious manner in a way they did not ask for, sexual assault occurs. Period.

And what about that most difficult form of sexual assault to define—the one that wears women down into finally giving in to sexual acts? Coercion seems to be the most difficult topic for our society to grasp. This happens most frequently when there is a large power imbalance between two people—when one person feels they have the right to not take no for an answer at any cost, and the other person agrees with this premise because of that person's stature.

Coercion is probably the largest problem we're facing in the battle to expand the definition of sexual assault, because it is so hard to prove. But there is also a certain amount of shame in admitting you were merely talked into doing something you didn't want to do, as opposed to being physically forced to do something you didn't want to do. I think a lot of women don't report being coerced into having sex because of this exact fear: that their reasoning sounds inexcusable and makes them come off as weak and unbelievable.

Which brings me to the second problem: our lack of justice not only for survivors, but for anyone who has experienced any form of abuse, neglect, intimidation, or trauma by someone in a position of power. One of the largest gifts this ignited era has brought us is the gift of showing survivors that there are, in fact, consequences not only for actions but for words. Until this moment in time, men in positions of power, and some women too, had gone virtually unchecked in their actions no matter their intentions.

My own husband had to deal with the consequences of what he perceived to be merely a joke made at the expense of a young Asian American comedian named Charlyne Yi. In his attempt to do an impression of a character he's been doing for decades in sketch comedy called Ronnie Dobbs, a Southern racist redneck the likes of which he grew up with in the South, he actually inflicted a racist act on Charlyne by using her physical body as the butt of the character's joke. When I heard about the situation, I was sickened but not shocked. Like many women, I can see how hard it is for men to realize where they are wrong. The accusation was very hard for David to grasp at first, and he fumbled his way through a terrible public apology to her in which he spelled her name wrong while simultaneously telling her she was probably misremembering the situation.

That word, *misremembering,* is something women are constantly being accused of by men, under many different circumstances, whether physical, mental, or emotional. Women are told they misremember all kinds of treatment—treatment that leaves lasting impressions and scars on many women's memories: from physical abuse, to sexual assault, to upsetting fights or disagreements with our male partners or peers, to disparaging and thoughtless remarks, to tasteless and insensitive jokes. David's cavalier use of this word *misremembering* was proof of his privilege— proof that he gets to handle things like most men in his position get to handle things: without much thought or care and at the total whim of his own feelings. He was blinded by his own despair at being accused of doing something he outright believed he did not do. He believed the encounter was not racist because he was doing an impression and it was a joke, in his mind. But racism transcends intention, and the only person who gets to decide whether it was in fact racist or not is Charlyne.

There was nothing I could do but be angry about the flippancy with which he responded to the situation and try to show him how wrong he was. With time and real patience on both of our parts, he came to understand how poorly he had handled things and would be the first one to tell you how wrong he was for doing it. But this would not be the last time he would use such bad judgment, and we have found ourselves in the situation that many heterosexual marriages are finding themselves in during this Era of Ignition—one of navigating very difficult conversations and seeing each other through our steepest of learning curves.

One afternoon David came home from a day of press for his television show *Arrested Development* looking pale, nervous, and gravely concerned. He proceeded to tell me that an interview with him and his cast members had gone very badly and he wasn't sure how it was going to be perceived. My heart sank. He didn't have to tell me what had happened in order for me to already know. David is and always has been a profoundly unique voice in the world of comedy, but his reaction to being questioned, accused, or implicated in hurtful behavior is a very ordinary one. I knew that he had likely said something damning during an interview, and I knew it likely pertained to his costar Jeffrey Tambor, a man who had recently been fired from the show *Transparent* for abusive behavior.

Regardless, I asked David what had happened and he told me, with much clarity, that their costar Jessica Walters had been brought to tears during a cast interview with the *New York Times* when speaking about the verbal abuse she had experienced on set from Mr. Tambor. But the worst of it was not that she had been brought to tears during the interview, it was that David and his male cast members had tried to give context to her story by defending Mr. Tambor and downplaying the experience as some sort of given—as behavior that is par for the course for any veteran on a television series. "It was really bad," he said to me, rubbing his head.

I looked him in the eye. He was right. It was really bad.

The public's reaction to the interview was a deserved scorch, leaving people so rightfully angry at the show's male cast members that the rest of their international press tour was canceled by Netflix overnight. Before I knew it, I too was swept up into the flames, with women tagging me on social media, asking me to comment, speak to, or explain my husband's interview. "You can't be a catalyst for the

#MeToo movement and not make a statement about what happened," read one woman's message to me. Others told me to divorce him, to deal with him, to come get him, or that he was canceled, or that I was canceled if I myself wouldn't cancel him.

I was sick about it for days and went off social media altogether. David, already prone to severe anxiety and depression from a young age, fell into one of the worst relapses of it I had ever seen. He didn't sleep and barely ate for weeks. He was horribly remorseful for the way it had gone down and how he contributed, and his despondency was made worse by the fury of women everywhere who had ever been a Jessica Walters in a room with entitled, inconsiderate men. I was extremely worried about David and his mental health and well-being during those weeks. And I was also worried for Jessica and how she might be feeling post-interview. David wrote Jessica and apologized for what had happened and I checked in on her, too. "I'm touched by people's responses," she wrote me back. "The world IS changing!"

In the time before this moment, it had long been my belief that women must not be held accountable or asked to speak for the actions of their male partners, a demand that is never asked of men regarding their female partners. To ask women to do so is a well-disguised form of misogyny, cloaked in an archaic allegiance to our gender archetypes. And while I've felt strongly about never breaking such restrictive molds for women, I know that things are not always that simple. I cannot remain silent for my belief's sake, especially now, when we need hard conversations to be had among women—to hear not just who women condemn publicly, but also what women will not condone or tolerate privately. I say this with the hope that the good men we love, who are not predators but problematic-adjacent, can learn and change from these experiences and no longer see them simply as blind spots, but as blind sight. Because what other choice is there for them than to learn how to see? This is the future and a matter of survival. And if they want to be a part of it, then they have to change along with it.

The difficult conversations I am having privately with my husband are the same conversations most women are having with their own male partners privately. I've heard it from countless women, from my own mother to famous actresses to women who approach me on the street. "How do we get through to them?" is the overall question. And the answer? They have to get through to themselves. We can show them the path, but it is up to them to take the journey.

These are hard, messy, and painful dialogues in marriages and partnerships, but they must take place. It's not fair to women, but it is a fact. Because the conversations I am having with my husband about what he's not seeing or doing to support women isn't the exception, it's the rule. And it's time we break it.

Like many women, I've been navigating the minefield of communication with men since 2017's #MeToo movement, most dishearteningly, with some of the most liberal men I know. It's been a constant exercise in patience and an unwillingness to waver on what I know to be true: that the world is heavily slanted in favor of men like my husband, which makes it so important that he not simply listen to the voices of women who have been silenced in a variety of ways, but that he really hear them, that he go out of his way to make sure they are being heard, at all costs—even at the cost of his own discomfort.

I love David with every fiber of my being. Even his blind spots. I believe he would say the same thing about me and my own failings. When we are disappointed or let down by each other, we dig in further and use the opportunity to better each other so that other people don't have to do it for us. Choosing to have these conversations together, however difficult, is not a burdened choice for me, as his wife, best friend, and partner of more than a decade. I believe in him, in that empathetic, complicated, curious, and inquisitive man I met all those years ago on an airplane headed to Shreveport, who I crashed so hard in love with and have come to understand and appreciate on such a richly complex level. I believe in his philosophical trajectory and his ability to transcend limitations for the sake of personal evolution. For the sake of finally seeing.

AT THE END OF 2017, a few months after millions of women told their stories of sexual harassment and assault across the world, my friend, the actor Ryan Reynolds, said to me, "I get it. I get what women are asking for right now. They would like us to back off and sit down and be quiet for a change while they figure out what they need. You don't need us giving you our opinions. You need us to take a time-out. Then once you've figured out what you need from us, you'll tell us, and we'll need to get on board and support you." I blinked rapidly and thought, *Yes, my favorite man-feminist, yes. That is exactly correct.*

Below is a Male Ally Manifesto for every kind of man, be it your boss, your friend, your partner, or your husband. Here are what I think are the five most important ways in which men can be proactive peers and help to create a more balanced world for women, but also for men.

1. Listen more than you assert. Read the emotional room and see what women need, not what you think they need based on your

opinions. Support the efforts for equality
and change being led by women—most
especially women of color and in the
LGBTQIA community. Let them lead the
charge; don't lead by taking charge.

2. No matter what your job title is, if there is a
woman in your field of work who is doing the
exact same job you are doing, tell her how
much money you make and then do something about it when you realize how much
more you are being paid. Men earn almost
double women's salaries and almost triple
the amount made by women of color. The pay
gap between genders and races in America
is indicative of the overall equality gap in
America, and one of the best ways men can
help level it out is by being transparent about
their income. Talk to your bosses about getting women additional pay, or support the
efforts of a woman in your field trying to get
paid more. Make space for women to be on
staff and make sure they are paid not just
what they deserve, but what their potential is,
the same way you would nurture young men's
potential. Ask your CEOs, your chairs, your
managers, your directors, your staffers to include women in their rooms.

3. If you see something, say something. If a woman is being harassed, bullied, or silenced in your presence, have a zero-tolerance policy. Don't tell yourself it's their problem to solve. Workplace harassment and assault can often be ended if someone of parallel privilege and power does something about it. Put your neck out on the line for those who, as Justice Ruth Bader Ginsberg once said, live with feet on their necks. When more women are in positions of power and there is equal representation in the room, there is less space for the abuse of power, physical or otherwise.

4. Put your money where your matriarchs are. Support organizations and causes that help to build and strengthen the next generation of women, from politics to creative writing. Organizations such as the Pink Door Writing Retreat, TWOCC (Trans Women of Color Collective), EMILY's List, Girls Rock, Time's Up, and Jack Jones Literary Arts, to name a few.

5. When it comes to men being accused of bad behavior, leave Sir William Garrow and his ancient law to the messy American justice system and instead listen to the rational and reasonable intelligence of women like Roxane Gay. On whether or not she believes

Woody Allen did or did not molest his daughter, Dylan Farrow, she once wrote: "I know where I stand and why. I know I would rather stand where I stand and eventually be proven wrong than support Woody Allen and eventually be proven wrong." In other words: Err on the side of women, not on the side of your brethren.

19

Looking back at those first months of 2017's #MeToo movement and the subsequent launch of Time's Up, I find myself asking what has changed, if anything. The answer is: Everything has changed.

Time's Up has become a global organization with real sustained power to affect legal and legislative policy, helping to stop workplace harassment and assault across industries and across the world. The #MeToo movement has made irreversible advancements in advocating for the rights and treatment of survivors of sexual assault through the powerful leadership and vision of Tarana Burke and those who have joined her efforts. Men have begun to not only step up as fierce advocates for women's rights and safety—men such as former NFL player Wade Davis, who has championed this moment in history by saying, "Here's what men don't get about the #MeToo movement. It's not about women, it's about us. Women are laying themselves bare for us to wake up." But men are also bravely stepping out to share their own stories of sexual assault and abuse, men like the actor Terry Crews, who testified about his own sexual harassment in front of the Senate Judiciary Committee to support the Sexual Assault Survivors' Rights Act.

One of my favorite initiatives to come out of the work that women have done within Time's Up is the +1 initiative, started by Desiree Gruber, founder and CEO of Full Picture. The +1 initiative was inspired by a desire to get more women into "the room where it happens" and the idea that you can't be what you can't see. This goes for young people first starting out in their careers, but it also applies to executives with hiring power: you can't recommend someone you've never met. This is the same idea I expressed to my friend Rebecca Carroll in a WNYC interview—the idea of having someone in your corner and lifting up another woman so that she is afforded the same opportunities you are. As Desiree says, "The idea behind +1 is to get more women out of the office and into the living, breathing, business matrix."

When I did the book tour for my novel, *Any Man*, I used the +1 initiative and invited all representations of women writers to join me, from trans to those with disabilities to women of color. It proved to be one of the most inspiring experiences of my entire life. I met powerful, bright new voices from authors I may not have otherwise been introduced to—authors like Rahne Alexander from Baltimore and Hilary Bell from Nashville and Jada Smith from Iowa City. It was an uplifting and eye-opening journey.

This +1 initiative that came out of Time's Up is not reserved just for me or anyone affiliated with the organization. It should be used by anyone and everyone, in any industry. It should be used by you, dear reader. There are many ways to apply it to what each of us does for a living, no matter what that might be. For instance, my own literary agent, Anthony Mattero, was so inspired by the idea of the +1 model that he asked me if his assistant Alex could join us for the pitches to publishers we would be making for the sale of this very book you are reading right now. Alex came with us to those meetings, and because of that experience and that access, Alex will forever know how a pitch meeting plays out, inside the room, should she ever find herself wanting to sell a book of her own someday. Besides the +1 model, the women and the men in Time's Up have worked across industry lines and class structures to amplify one another's work and make sure that each of us is using the best of what we have to offer in order to leave a better future for everyone's children, boys and girls alike.

I think back to this ignited era's first year and all the incredible moments I have experienced working alongside women and men who have dedicated their entire lives to keeping this burning revolution fueled so that we never have to return to a time when our bodies and experiences are evaporating concerns. One of the greatest experiences I had along the way was just before the Golden Globes in early 2018 when a small group of women from Time's Up sat down with Tarana Burke. We were very fortunate to have her guidance and experience with regard to the statement we wanted to make at the Globes—a statement both visual and intentional, sending a message of solidarity between women of all kinds. We unified by wearing black and speaking out candidly on the injustices facing all industries, free from the usual glimmering filter of the red carpet's vapidity. For actresses, this was a revolutionary moment that released us from the notion that our bodies are mere rentable hooks on which to hang clothing and sell fashion. The conformity forced interviewers and the media to talk to us about who we were bringing as our guests, not just what we were wearing.

The night the Globes took place, we threw Sisters in Solidarity parties on the West and East Coasts, and Uzo Aduba and I hosted the one in New York. Reese Witherspoon was one of the most instrumental women in that journey, and she worked tirelessly to make sure that the evening had something substantive to say and that every gender that was attending, male or female, was invited to be a part of what we were fighting for—that our declaration at an award show like the Golden Globes was not just a moment in history, but a moment in the long-term revolution.

In Uzo's living room, we gathered together and watched as our sisters arrived on the red carpet, arm-in-arm, speaking forcefully and eloquently about the problems women face in every industry across the country. Women like activists Rosa Clemente, Saru Jayaraman, Marai Larasi, Ai-jen Poo, and Mónica Ramírez spoke to reporters who usually ask questions pertaining to clothes and jewelry about the injustices facing immigrant women, women working in factories, in restaurants, and in our fields. It felt freeing and invigorating to watch as each extraordinary woman took center stage on the carpet during one of America's most superficial evenings. We screamed and applauded for our sisters on television, but none so much as when Oprah Winfrey said in her Lifetime Achievement Award speech, "For too long, women have not been heard or believed if they dared to speak their truth to the power of those men. But their time is up." It is an experience I will never forget: a proclamation that rippled through the television into living rooms everywhere, into our nation's ears and the world's minds—an inspired invocation for us all.

While actions like the 2018 Golden Globes can feel small and insignificant in hindsight, they are one of many sparks that have created a cumulative change in the way much of our culture views the priority of protecting women's bodies. This is just the beginning. And the work we all must keep doing will be unrelenting and exhausting at times. And surely we will fail sometimes as we continue to learn and grow. However difficult, modest, or insignificant these small changes may feel in a world largely ready for a drastic shift, our achievements should be seen as the laying of new pavement—a fresh foundation on which we will build a better future for all kinds of people.

In the last year, we have seen an unprecedented uprising from women across the globe, from South African women protesting to end gender-based discrimination and violence, to the international walkout of Google employees protesting the company's handling of sexual assualt cases, to hundreds of thousands marching in Switzerland to end the gender pay gap. None of these milestones are insignificant and each one, voice by voice, ignition after ignition, is changing the landscape of how we will coexist in this world, boldly and without fear. Remember: Rome wasn't built and then burned to the ground in a day, and neither will dismantling a system that has persecuted marginalized voices since the beginning of time be accomplished quickly. Our endurance to break through the barriers must out-last their determination to keep us where we are. Let those abusing their power keep going with their talks of witch hunts, their diminishing of our move-ments, their death-rattle dog whistles. Our response will never be unheard, ignored, or silenced again.

20

The question all parents ask themselves is: What kind of world have I brought my child into? I wonder if my own mother ever felt that way about me. I recently texted her during a bout of depression and asked, "Mom, when you were pregnant with me, did you ever think to yourself: What kind of world am I bringing this poor girl into?" My mother responded by saying, "No. We were delighted to have you. There was hope then—especially for environmental concerns—but now we have reached that fateful tipping point that many scientists warned us about. As a species, we have fouled the nest. Now it's about adapting and building supportive villages. We might get lucky and some brilliant team can invent a carbon capture technology . . . but we will be fine. Marlow will be fine. Many good years left to live. Take heart."

While I have no idea what survivalist malarkey that "carbon capture technology" was about (bless California hippies), I did understand her and feel relief from her words. As a new mother to my daughter, Marlow, I have been no different in my fears. But I've started to focus like my mother focuses: less on the world I have brought my daughter into and more on the world I will be leaving for her—by fighting to change it. It is a test of true perseverance. After having Marlow, I was thrust from my own self-centered wallowing into a sort of permanent projectile optimism. As difficult as things are and as impossible as that sounds, I am not without what sometimes feels like supernatural hope—the sorcery of promise, the magic of Making It So. I try to visualize the world's transformation and see my daughter as something budding from its abundance, not suffering in its stagnancy. Every quaking nerve, every rattled premonition, every fear for the future propels my indignation into action. And my daughter carries within her now that sparked gene.

But while she is of my being, she does not belong to me, and her freedom from my physical body presents a terrifying fact most parents face: I cannot control her safety. There is ultimately nothing I can do to fully protect her from this world. So instead of worrying about that all the time (which I do), I aim to change the world instead. I know it's a wholly unreasonable desire, but it is the only choice I've got. That any of us have.

The world I want to give her will be safe and fair and representative of all bodies, not just the ones that look like her own. It will be wild and riveting and full of tender wonder and sometimes failure. It will be intentioned and imperfect, but not imbalanced. And it will still be complicated, unfair at times, and disappointing—the world will be a ferocious verse sung into a universe of similar songs. It will be filled with more possibility than passivity. More empathy than sympathy. The world I want to give her will be a leap into the riot of her own imagination. I want her to see with as much desire as she longs to be seen. To listen to others with as much focus as she longs to be heard. I want her to never have to be afraid to be in a room alone with someone, whether for work or for love. The world I want to give her has no mirrors to bully her frame, no scales meant to shame her size, no culture nurtured to reject her voice. It will love her, unabridged. And it will teach her to respect others, uncategorically.

The world I want to give Marlow is the one we are living in, reborn—one that is nourished, healed, and flourishing; one that is courageous, compassionate, and full of grace; one that is done with the vortexes of harm's haunting, done with the celebrated parades of pain and the sick cyclicality of American callousness. I want to give her a world where love is a given and innocence is not a virtue to be taken. A world of her choosing, not a world already chosen.

I want this for your children, too, and for our universe's children—most especially for our planet Earth and her Sister in Solidarity, Saturn, whose big, bruising, everlasting return will forever be felt by us as long as humans are living. I want our children to grow up in unison, but each with their own individual uniqueness, like the atoms of water in a river, unpredictable, independent, charged, and free. I can see it now: my daughter's entire life on the horizon, like a sun glaring on the glass of the ocean's surface; her waves impermanent, her salt spectacular, the body of her owning the moon's pull. I can see it now: my girl's trajectory of curiosity, kindness, and dignity, vibrating alongside every other drop of human life.

SEE THEM AND SPEAK to them with me now: our children and their futures, the children of our friends and family, flooding with actualization, reverberating all the light we have ever relit and all the births we will ever gift.

Epilogue

Dear Marlow,

There are many different kinds of floods. There are the floods of hormones, of emotions, of memories. The flash flood, the overbank, the urban, and the coastal flood. There are flood warnings and flood watches. Catastrophic floods and the flooding of markets. There is the flood of tears, the flood of phone lines, and, of course, flood insurance. There is psychotherapeutic flooding and the flooding of an engine. The biblical, the metaphysical, the metaphorical, and the astronomical. And behind every flood is a fracturing. A dam that gave out, or an ocean's swell that came in, or a pipe that burst, or a mind that shattered, or a heart that cracked. Behind every flood is a cause, a consuming that can no longer be contained; a river overflowing, a volcano erupting, a collective conscious writhing, a vibration pulsing. And then there is you: young daydreamer of the deluge, pulp of prescience, torrent of radical instinct, my child, my love.

Right now, your young mind is an erupting body of feral water, ready to soak up the world around you. You've been on this planet for only two years, but you are beginning to understand how complicated it is, equal parts cruel, unfair, and filled with joyous light. Your young power, your fresh perception—your potential—will someday pierce the soft banks of your living and you will flow into who you were meant to be, no matter the gender you arrive at, the heart you pound with, the voice you conquer the world with.

My hope for you is a hope for every child who comes into this world. That you are seen by this world as not just a single flame, but as the fire that forged your own way. No matter the pain, no matter the consequence, no matter the failure, I hope you emerge true to what you want, not just true to who you are. I know that sometimes you will feel lost because I too have felt lost. Sometimes life can make you feel like you are something received rather than reciprocated. But this I can promise: one day you will be seen and valued for the depths of your riverbed, not just the clarity of your water. For the crash of your gush, not just the speed of your tide. Your very existence is the declaration of an untamed instinct, wild and indomitable, tangled and fueled for this breaking open, this pushing through, this era and its most untamable ignition.

But none of this will come without years of undoing first—without years of being undone. I will give you everything I have and everything I know as your mom, and that will still not be enough. And it might also still be wrong. I will do my best to bring you to the river's edge, but you must find your own way to float. You will have to fight and undo the ways you were taught, by me and the world, and also fight to continue to learn on your own. You will have to undo hesitation, creative hibernation, and the casting of your furnace as a caricature to be outsourced. You will spend many moons hearing people tell you that this instinct, this knowing, this oracle of your gut, will forever be both your blessing and your curse.

But here is the secret, Marlow: For women, there's no such thing as a curse. Curses are for fractured kings and clocks that forever tick backward. Curses are for the contexts of hexing. And you cannot be implicated; your instincts will never be conquered, they can only be conjured.

COME CLOSE. BE HERE with me now, in this body that is your own, in this grown space where our shared skin is the binding of our story. One day when you are grown and I am gone, I want you to remember this letter, this offering as a way into the flood of who you will become—of what you were put here on this earth to do. Remember that the anxiety you'll inevitably feel someday, the isolation you will carry, the stories you will tell, and the silence you will store is not part of some curse. It is part of your dawning. Your doing. A Saturn Return, a revolution inside you, a motivation to swell.

This world can be tough. This world can be unkind and confused and filled with people who mean to do harm, or even who don't but still do it anyway. This world may leave you feeling as lost as a locket in the ocean, as raw as a skinned heart, as withheld from yourself as I ever did. To find yourself in it, pull the pin on your instincts and detonate. Watch what collapses, what bursts, what is forced to break out. Be propelled into your journey and the journey of others, forever linking arms with the arteries of kindred hearts. Beat in cadence, a rhythm for change. Because we are all just the flooding of blood into a single flow, into one solitary fuel, hoping for a pulse, one profound pounding at a time.

Love,
Mom

Afterword

A few months after handing in the final draft of this book to my editor at the end of 2018, a monumental historic event took place. One after another, an unprecedented number of women announced their candidacy for president of the United States in the 2020 presidential election. Senator Kamala Harris, a former prosecutor from California, was the first to announce, followed by Senator Elizabeth Warren, a former law school professor, until a record six women had entered the race before a single male candidate had. This increase in representation ushered in one of the most powerful shifts in the cultural landscape—one that most men have taken for granted, and women (and other marginalized people) have largely been denied: the matter of choice.

AFTERWORD

One of America's most sacred values is the privilege of having choices; whether selecting political candidates, educators, or physicians, we are given options to inform our decision-making. The problem is, those options are limited. Most men have always been able to see different versions of themselves represented in positions of power, which is why the argument "The best candidate should get the job, regardless of their gender" is problematic, because the measurement for what is considered "the best" has, up until recently, been reserved for those exclusive few. Cis men, especially cis white men, have always had the luxury of being able to choose or be chosen by other men just like them, and because of this foundational freedom, they often overlook the importance of what having choice might mean for other people who do not have it as freely. Because most men have never had to protect choice in the same way women have, they often don't see it as something with a shelf life—as something that can be taken from them at any moment. That's why the very act of these six highly qualified women running for president was a necessary reminder of the importance of choice, both personal and professional.

Now that we have a plurality of both men *and* women candidates running for president, their individual values and what they each bring to the table can be weighed fairly, instead of weighing a single woman candidate against a pack of advantaged male peers. Having women to choose from allows us to have discussions and make informed decisions about who really *is* the best candidate for the job. And while this is a start, we still need even more representation in future election cycles—trans women, women with disabilities, Native American women—to have a substantive debate about policy. When you have real representation, you have better results, because the choice you are making is one built on equality, and an equal playing field makes for an equal match. You wouldn't want to watch a sports game where the outcome was rigged in favor of one team over the other, would you? The same logic should apply for the person who will be running our country.

Even with all the women running for president, an air of sexism still permeates the current political landscape, a by-product of the patriarchal spell that has been cast over us for far too long, begging to be broken. It is a spell that says: We love that so many women are running, but we don't believe any of them can win. We love all the women candidates, but Kamala Harris is too tough and untrustworthy a stateswoman. (And Joe Biden is not?) We love all the women candidates, but Elizabeth Warren is too scolding and angry. (And Bernie Sanders is not?) We love all the women candidates, but who is Kirsten Gillibrand anyway, and why does she remind me of my mother-in-law? This narrative seems to play out in every kind of political election like clockwork: *Of course* we want a woman to be president someday, just not *that* woman. Or that one. That woman is also not quite right. She's too emotional. No, sorry, she won't do either. She's irritating. Or her. She also won't do. Or her. Nope. Sorry. No.

While we are seeing more diverse choices now as far as our political candidates are concerned, we have yet to overcome our national wariness to actually *choose* one of them—to elect a woman to be president. The American media doesn't always help the fight to destigmatize women's political legitimacy either, and they often end up writing think pieces or opinion articles that support such dangerous narratives about women politicians. So many major news outlets in 2019 shared similar sexist headlines that I found myself imagining how ridiculous the titles would sound had they been about the male opponents in the race. Imagine if this *New York Times* headline was about a man instead of a woman: "Asked If a *Man* Can Win, 2020 Candidates Offer an Easy Answer: 'I Have.'" Or this one from NBC News: "Can a *Man* Beat Trump? Some Democrats Wonder If It's Worth the Risk." Risk. Uncertainty. Danger. These are all words used to describe women as liabilities rather than assets; as if women are professionally unworthy or incapable of being as invested as men always have been.

Rhetoric like this just adds fuel to the flames that have been burning down women's credibility for generations. The media perpetuates this fear of choosing the wrong candidate by citing the only other example they have: Hillary Clinton. And herein lies the problem. When we haven't had long-term representation, when we haven't had different women to choose from for as long as men have had different men to choose from, we fall back on sexist, gendered clichés because we know no other route. Elizabeth Warren was often asked how she was going to escape being "Hillary'd" during her run, or if she thought a woman could actually win. But the fact remains, Hillary Clinton is absolutely nothing like the women running for president in the 2020 election, and they are nothing like her.

While we do have a few choices now as far as presidential candidates are concerned, our rights to personal choices as women are being rolled back cruelly and recklessly, most especially pertaining to women's health care. In the middle of 2019, the state of Georgia introduced the Heartbeat Bill, which bans women from getting abortions and even goes so far as prosecuting them if they attempt to get the procedure done in another state. Subsequently, more than nine states introduced similarly oppressive laws, which left an overwhelming fear that *Roe v. Wade* might be next on the chopping block. Only in America can you see the groundbreaking advancement of choices for women in their professional lives followed by laws that ban the choices for women in

their personal ones. We have always been a hypocritical nation, holding dear our personal freedoms
while strangling the rights of others—none so much
as the right of women to make decisions for their
own bodies.

Most of these states and their bills are aimed
toward stopping *late-term abortion*, a phrase that
is more of a political construct than a real medical
definition. In fact, any obstetrician would tell you
the phrase was just an invention by pro-life activists meant to purposefully mislead by omitting real
information about why, exactly, these types of abortions are taking place. The so-called pro-life movement makes no mention of fetuses that are so severely
compromised by organ anomalies that they will very
likely not survive a full pregnancy term. Anomalies such as anencephaly, which is the absence of the
development of a major part of the fetus's brain and
skull, or hydrops, a sometimes fatal condition where
large amounts of fluid build up in the fetal tissue,
causing extreme swelling. These are just a few of the
very real reasons why women must sometimes have
an abortion further into a pregnancy than expected.

Recently, I spoke to twenty-six-year veteran obstetrician Dr. Karen Kirsch about these new laws
and what they mean in practical terms for women
and their choices.

"The term *partial-birth abortion* is a fallacy," Dr.
Kirsch told me recently over the phone. "This is a

procedure that does not exist. *Late-term abortion* is vague and unclear and allows the anti-abortion faction to detract from the greater truth and underlying problem: This is about class, predominantly affecting the poor. This is about women who do not have access or the financial means to obtain the adequate prenatal health they deserve in a timely fashion. This means, for example, women do not get to obtain early sonograms that can pick up severe fetal anomalies not compatible with life, such as anencephaly, so they seek terminations later in pregnancy. The same can be said for women who have a worsening serious underlying medical problem endangering their lives. I assume this is what is meant by *late-term abortion*."

As far as a woman's right to make decisions for herself when it comes to such personal matters, Dr. Kirsch said, "That's the importance of the choice factor. A woman could carry to term with an abnormal fetus and deal with the aftermath at birth, or risk dying if she has a severe medical issue. But that has to remain her choice and no one else's. The assault on choice, which is nothing new but sadly escalating, must be challenged."

Indeed, phrases like *partial-birth abortion* and *late-term abortion* aim to make it the government's business, focusing solely on the three terms of gestation during pregnancy, and therefore, the life of the fetus only, all but erasing the needs of the woman whose life will forever be impacted by the repercussions of that pregnancy. The phrase is born out of the folklore of anti-abortion extremists, invoking visions of cute little babies with thumping heartbeats getting "ripped from the mother's womb before birth," as President Donald Trump once said of late-term abortions at a rally. It is meant to make abortion sound like a simplified subject: death by murder. My question is: Who gets to define what death is in the first place? Or life, for that matter? Is it religion? Is it the government? Or is it doctors? Or women whose bodies are the subjects of such questions?

Most of what is understood about abortions and why women choose them is morbidly mythologized, painting the worst possible picture of arbitrary decisions on life and death. Even the language around people's beliefs is aimed to fabricate truth: People who believe abortion is murder call themselves "pro-life," even though for many women, having an abortion could actually save their lives. The idea of "saving lives" is reserved for the innocence of "unborn children" (a debatable and highly misleading phrase to use in this circumstance), but child immigrants currently locked up in concentration camps on our southern borders seemingly do not qualify. So what of the very real, very innocent, very young immigrant children who have died in American custody already in 2019? Where are the conservative men and women lawmakers and so-called pro-lifers who are outraged and pushing for a Heartbeat Bill for these young refugees?

The term *pro-life* assumes that the rest of us are simply pro-death. This notion that women are murdering their babies purposefully paints women as bad choice makers, as people incapable of knowing what's *right* in the first place, and therefore, incapable of making any other choices either. Presidential candidate Pete Buttigieg once said of the debate on term limits for abortion, "I think the dialogue has gotten so caught up on when you draw the line that we've gotten away from the fundamental question of who gets to draw the line. And I trust women to draw the line." He went on to say that most women who have to have an abortion later on in their pregnancy usually have to make a very painful decision for medical reasons. "We're talking about women who have perhaps chosen the name, women who have purchased the crib, families that then get the most devastating medical news of their lifetimes, something about the health or the life of the mother that forces them to make an impossible, unthinkable choice. That decision [to have an abortion] is not going to be made any better, medically or morally, because the government is dictating how that decision should be made."

I have known many women—and I do mean *many*—who have had to make unthinkable yet very thought-out choices at every stage of a pregnancy. Many of us have also felt great relief from having the choice to do with our bodies what we feel—what we *know*—is right for us at that time. Expanding our choices and freeing us up to decide what is best for ourselves—for our bodies, our families, our futures—is something that will benefit all of us in the long run.

I look at women like Janet Mock who, in 2019, became the first trans woman to get an overall deal at a major studio (Netflix) and now has the freedom to choose which stories she wants to tell to enrich the intelligence and perspectives of television viewers. Her freedom to make new creative choices will only enrich us as a culture. Similarly, New York State passed an unprecedented and powerful bill, led by lawyer Roberta Kaplan for Time's Up, called the New York Safety Agenda, which lifts the statute of limitations for people who want to report second- and third-degree rape. This new law gives people more time to choose when they are ready to report a sexual assault, instead of forcing them to do so simply because their story has an expiration date according to the justice system. It is precisely this expansion of choices for women and marginalized voices that will continue changing the trajectory of our country for the better.

I'll end here, dear reader, by asking you to join me in taking action as we move into this new era of making choices and having choices. Look around at your community, at your family, at your friendships and partnerships, and ask yourself two questions: What does choice look like for you and what does it look like for other people? And what can you do to create choices for others where there are none? This isn't about fighting to empower other people; we are already the arbiters of our own sorcery, each of us fueled by our own individual fires. So instead of fighting for empowerment, I will ask you to fight for freedom, and not just your own. The freedom to love. The freedom to vote. The freedom to live. The freedom to choose and be chosen.

Acknowledgments

Thank you to the matriarchal lines on both sides of my family who built the foundation of who I am, through blood first: my sister, China, my mom, Bonnie, my aunts, Glenda, Carrie, and Alexandra. Thank you to my grandmothers, Sally and Marian Alice. Thank you to the women who bore them and the women before that.

Thank you to my Sisters in Solidarity, both new and old. To all the women in Time's Up, across industries: I'm honored to work alongside all of you. Thank you to the sisters who have informed so much of who I am today: Mindy Nettifee, Rachel McKibbens, April Jones, Leslie Silva, Emily Wells, Samantha Nye, Rebecca Carroll, Katie Jacobs, Laura Prepon, Lidia Yuknavitch, and Roxane Gay. Thank you to Phillip Picardi and *Teen Vogue* as well as Rachel Dry and the *New York Times*.

Thank you to the women who contributed their time and voices to this book, both anonymously and by name and with pen. Much gratitude for the friendships and writing of Airea D. Matthews and Meredith Talusan.

Thank you to the teams who nurtured this book, starting with my literary agent, Anthony Mattero. Thank you to my extraordinary editor, Tricia Boczkowski, and to Kathryn Santora, Rachel Aldrich, and the whole PR team at Crown Archetype. Special shout-out to Jennifer Schuster.

Thank you, team ID-PR, Alla Plotkin, Amanda Pelletier, and Jillian Roscoe, as well as the amazing Nancy Gates at UTA. Thank you to those who nurtured my foundation from the beginning: Laurel Schmidt, Joan Hyler, Harris Hartman, Jack Hirschman, and my father, Russ.

Much gratitude for those who aided in the research for this book, including the Annenberg Foundation and Lillian Soderman for her analytics and research of statistics, as well as Audrey Gelman and The Wing for giving me space to write every day.

I am extremely grateful for the healers and teachers and supporters who made the writing of this book possible. Thank you, Evan, John, Vickie Lee, Dr. Mary Banyo, Lisa Love, and, most especially, Stacy Armoogan.

ACKNOWLEDGMENTS

Thank you to my husband, David. For more than I can possibly put into words here. I love you.

This book is also dedicated to the memory and writing of Wanda Coleman and my sister, America Ferrera.

About the Author

Amber Tamblyn is an author, actress, and director. She's been nominated for an Emmy, a Golden Globe, and an Independent Spirit Award for her work in television and film, including *House, M.D.* and *The Sisterhood of the Traveling Pants*. She is the author of four books, including the bestseller *Dark Sparkler* and the critically acclaimed novel *Any Man*. Tamblyn cowrote and directed for Netflix the feature film *Paint It Black,* based on the novel by Janet Fitch, starring Alia Shawkat, Janet McTeer, and Alfred Molina. She reviews books of poetry by women for *Bust* magazine and is poet in residence at Amy Poehler's Smart Girls. In addition Tamblyn is a founding member of Time's Up and a contributing writer for the *New York Times.* She lives in New York.

ERA OF IGNITION

ESSAYS,
READER'S GUIDES,
AND MORE

A Reader's Guide for *Era of Ignition* by Amber Tamblyn

Questions and Topics for Discussion

1. An Era of Ignition, according to the author, is "a thriving time of condensed evolution, where many discourses about who we are and the difficult dialogues about where we are going kick into high gear" (page 11). What does this term mean to you?

2. Have you experienced your own Era of Ignition? What impact do you think it had on your life, your relationships, or you as an individual?

3. In the author's attempts to adapt and direct Janet Fitch's *Paint It Black,* she experienced numerous roadblocks and felt that her work was often unfairly compared to the work of men. Where else have you seen examples of this in your life or in the lives of those around you?

4. Women, according to the author, "are raised to doubt first and decide last" (page 15). Does this resonate with you? Why or why not? Do you see a way in which you can change this mindset in yourself or in someone close to you?

5. Desiree Gruber of the Time's Up organization created the "+1 initiative," meant to give individuals who might not be afforded the same opportunities as others the chance to take part in important conversations and be in the "room where it happens" (page 240). How do you feel you fit into the +1 model? Do you have something to offer others based on your own experiences, or do you feel that you would benefit from being the +1 person? Can you list five women who you could help support with the access you might have in your life? Or can you name five women who could possibly do this for you?

6. The author has her own "Male Ally Manifesto" (pages 235–38) describing the ways in which men can be proactive peers for women. How else do you think men can best be allies of women? How would you personally go about being a better ally of women, or how would you suggest the men in your life become better allies?

7. The author describes a time in which she had to explain to her husband how his actions had

been hurtful to women, and how he could learn and change from the experience. She acknowledges that it's "not fair to women" that they have to lead these difficult conversations with the men in their lives but also argues the conversations "must take place" (page 233). Do you agree that women have an obligation to lead these conversations? Do you feel it is a burden? Why or why not?

8. The author addresses the issue of "white feminism" (page 171) and acknowledges the ways in which she has contributed to it in the past. How have you taken part in or been impacted by white feminism in your life?

9. What are some concrete ways that individuals can work to make their feminism intersectional? What can you do personally to open the discussion to those who might otherwise be left out?

10. Before giving birth to her daughter, the author asks, "How do we encourage and support our daughters by talking to them and making them feel powerful without lying to them about the realities of the world we live in" (page 66)? What are some ways to have these kinds of conversations with the next generation? Is there someone in your life who you can support in this way?

A Conversation
with Amber Tamblyn

Q. You've been very active as a writer, with published op-eds, a novel (*Any Man*) and various poetry collections (*Free Stallion, Bang Ditto, and Dark Sparkler*) under your belt. Was your writing process any different this time around?

A. I think the process of writing these scenes, which are so personal, and a nonfiction book altogether, was far more difficult than I had anticipated. Mostly because I wasn't ready to go into the raw and difficult subject matter of my own personal journey growing up as an actress. With most of my other writing, I am merely using my imagination to create worlds that aren't real, or are real-adjacent. It's quite another thing to talk about the literal truth in that way. The experience gave me quite a newfound respect for memoirists.

Q. How long have you been thinking about/ working on the content of *Era of Ignition*?

A. I started thinking about this book during the presidential election in 2016. I was trying to formulate how I felt about this time in our culture, which consists of so much rapid, condensed change—change that often comes in the form of a lot of intense clashing and rehashing of old cultural wounds. I wanted to explore the idea of an entire country's existential crisis, and the awakening that comes after that, which I believe we are in now. This is nothing new for our country: It's a cycle that comes and goes, as new issues arise and new challenges are faced. Once Donald Trump was elected, I knew I had to write this book. And it came out of me like a Dwayne Johnson franchise: Fast. And. Furious.

Q. *Era of Ignition* delves into personal and low periods in your life. You show parts of yourself that are vulnerable and unguarded, and you are unflinchingly and unapologetically honest. Tell us about the moment you decided you wanted to share these parts of yourself with the world.

A. I don't know if it was ever a decision really; I just felt propelled into the writing by sheer proximity to the insanity of the world we live in today. I felt that if I didn't share my own stories, and also make the larger connection to a world and culture deep in the midst of its own existential crisis, then I wouldn't truly be contributing to the larger conversation.

Q. Which story are you most looking forward to sharing with the world?

A. I'm very excited to have more nuanced conversations about what people feel like they are missing from this world and to hear about their own personal eras of ignitions: When was the last time you had an existential crisis? And what was the result of that experience? How did you get motivated after it? What have you been doing with your anger in this Donald Trump world? So many questions!

Q. Of the essays in *Era of Ignition*, which do you most wish you could share with yourself at a younger age? What age?
A. I think the letter to my daughter could really be applied to my child self in many ways. I wrote the original draft as such—a letter to my inner child. I hope and think that it will resonate with a lot of people, whether or not they have children. Because we all have a child inside of us we must protect, still, even as adults.

Q. You also talk about your activism work as one of the founders of the Time's Up organization, as well as your fight for equality, intersectional feminism, and women's rights. You aren't afraid to address the difficult and tough topics of the time. Why is releasing a book like this important?
A. I think honesty is never the problem with books like these. Mining for new and more complicated honesty is what's so crucial in this world right now. We must be having difficult conversations with ourselves and with others. We must ask not just how we can help others, but also find out how we may have hurt others. The only way to grow as a society is to

face these things head-on. To not hold tightly to our beliefs and defensiveness but rather to be open to all forms of dialogue that aim to heal and aim to expand us. It is in the dialogue where we will find the change we so desperately are looking for, not the cherishing of our interior monologues. I hope this book is a dialogue for people. I hope it is not just absorbed but elicits response.

Q. You also note that while we are in this intense time of questioning and reckoning, what follows is an era of ignition that "fires up the answers," so who are some people (writers, activists, etc.) who you feel are leading us in the right direction? And who do you hope to see leading the country in more official capacities in the next few years?

A. Such a good question! I always think about the writers in our culture first. Brittney C. Cooper, who wrote *Eloquent Rage,* Rebecca Traister, Claudia Rankine. And I am, of course, watching all the historic and unprecedented number of women running for president already. It fills me with so much joy and a strong sense of calm, knowing that our fate might end up in the hands of a woman. Finally. I would also say it's very important to follow the women activists who are revolutionizing systems of oppression: Mónica Ramírez, Ai-Jen Poo, Saru Jayaraman, to name a few. These are women changing the nation one powerful action at a time. Know them. Follow them.

Q. If you were to build a reading list, a primer of sorts, for women sparking change and leading the revolution, where would you suggest readers start? (Feminist fiction, nonfiction, and poetry, perhaps with themes around resistance, resilience, and activism are all welcome!) And which female authors have inspired you over the years?

A. I've named a few above, but I would also include the poetry of Erika L. Sánchez, Mindy Nettifee, Franny Choi, Rachel McKibbens, and Patricia Smith. I would read work by Esmé Wang, Beau Sia, and Ijeoma Oluo as well. There's also Lucille Clifton, Diane di Prima, Sharon Olds, Lidia Yuknavitch, Toni Morrison, Randa Jarrar, and Samantha Irby. And I feel like I say this a lot, but perhaps it can't be said enough: Read the work of Audre Lorde. All of it. Every word.

Q. **Do book tours bring anything new to your work with Time's Up?**

A. The tours have been so great to connect with people who want to be involved on a personal level and in their own communities. I've met so many different kinds of people, from different walks of life, with such strong ideas for how they can work to change their own communities for the better. This is truly the spirit of how Time's Up was formed: That each of us has the power to create real and lasting change when we get together with like minds and we stop asking for permission to make that change happen.

Q. If nothing else, what is one thing you hope readers take away from your memoir?

A. I hope you are refueled for the fight to protect yourself and your creative value in this world, but also refueled to fight those who aim to withhold such freedoms from any person. I hope the book helps you tap into your own era of ignition; a time of condensed and powerful change.